Mallard Ducks

The Comprehensive Mallard Duck Guide Book

by

Harry Goldcroft

DISCLAIMER

This book is intended for information and educational purposes only. While every attempt has been made to verify the facts and information provided herein, neither the author nor publisher assumes any responsibility for errors, inaccuracies or omissions, and specifically disclaim any implied warranties or merchantability or fitness for any particular purpose and shall in no event be liable for any loss of profit or any other commercial damage, including but not limited to special, incidental, consequential, or other damages.

In addition, neither the author nor publisher makes any guarantees, including but not limited to any express or implied endorsement of any the organizations, sites or other references listed in this book as resources for further information, assistance, equipment, or other uses. And the reader expressly assumes all risk in dealing with these sources. Furthermore, while accurate at the time of original publication, due to the ever changing nature of the internet and the world we live in addresses, links, urls, phones numbers and/or individual contact persons may not have changed.

Any slights of people or organizations are unintentional.

This book was printed in the UK and USA.

COPYRIGHT

PIB Publishing
13 Pencross View
Hemyock
Cullompton
Devon. EX15 3XH
United Kingdom

Dedication

To all those lovers of these magnificent ducks

Table of Contents

Chapter One: Introduction

The concept of domesticating animals is not new; we have been forging bonds with animals in order to co-exist peacefully since the beginning of time. While earlier civilizations taught us to breed cattle, horses and poultry for personal consumption and profit, our relationship with the animal kingdom today has become more complex, even emotional.

We now view animals, not only as a source of profit, but also as a source of love and companionship. What is interesting to note, however, is that people tend to have varied preferences when asked to select an animal they would like to house.

For some people, the perfect animal companion is one that is energetic, affectionate and boisterous. Those with a quiet demeanour may prefer an animal that is well-behaved, disciplined and calm. Some may describe their perfect companions to be those who swim behind large glass enclosures, providing tranquillity and beauty. And some others still may choose to bring home those pets that can be trained and raised for long-term profits. If you belong to that elite group of people who likes their pets to have a little of all the above qualities, Mallard ducks may be the pets you've been looking for!

Mallard ducks are quirky, fascinating creatures. Known throughout the animal kingdom for being sticklers for routine and schedules, Mallard ducks are surprisingly ill-suited for house training. There is historical evidence that reveals interaction between humans and Mallard ducks for a few hundred years at least, and yet they can be highly suspicious of their owners. Known to be aloof and detached, Mallard ducks may one day become dissatisfied with the settings you provide and choose to simply fly away. Such is the nature of these proud birds. Given the right setting, however, these semi-aquatic birds can become a calm - if messy - addition to your household.

As comfortable as they may seem in domestic settings, Mallard ducks are just at ease in a wild environment. With strong defence mechanisms, an aggressive attitude and a penchant for breeding, Mallard ducks tend to thrive in their natural environments.

The purpose behind bringing home Mallard ducks greatly influences the method through which they are raised. While they may make ideal lifelong companions, Mallard ducks are also a prized source of both meat and eggs in many parts of the world. Mallard ducks reared as food sources are raised in different conditions compared to their domestic counterparts.

Many Mallard duck owners will refrain from raising their ducks for meat, but will certainly use the copious amount of eggs for personal use or profit. Whatever be the ultimate goal, raising Mallard ducks requires a commitment to keeping the birds as healthy and stress-free as possible.

Being creatures of habits and highly sensitive to change, Mallard ducks will require extra work on the owner's part to ensure their safety and well-being. Indeed, certain conditions that make an environment habitable for Mallard ducks can stretch well beyond human capabilities. When you can determine the best conditions within which to house the ducks, rest assured that the ducks will live to become loyal companions.

As tempting as they may look at your local fair, or pet vendor's, the care required to keep a Mallard duck far exceeds their attractiveness. You may bring home a duckling on a whim, only to find that your living conditions don't favour a Mallard duck in the least. Some ducks that are purchased impulsively also find themselves abandoned in public parks and streams. Since the Mallard duck requires their community to survive, this regretful purchase could turn out to be traumatic for the duck.

The compatibility of your surroundings with the duck is also important as Mallard ducks interact in many direct and indirect ways with the ecology. If they are the dominant species in an area, they are likely to wipe it off all visible flora and fauna, before looking for more spots to forage. This natural instinct may not be beneficial to you, especially if you live in an urban setting.

Discipline and routine will also play very important parts in shaping the lifestyle of your Mallard ducks. Prone to a unique concept called imprinting, Mallard ducklings may adopt you as their caregiver, and need you to provide them with food and shelter till they are adults.

It is for these reasons that deliberation and careful consideration are key when deciding whether you want to bring home a Mallard duck. You will also have to understand that the arrival of a new species in your household impacts not only your lives, but the life of the duck as well. It is important that the Mallard receive fair treatment from all those they interact with - be it your family members, or other domestic animals.

The interaction between your ducks and animals such as your pet dogs becomes especially crucial if the ducks are brought to start an animal husbandry endeavour. Through healthy interaction with other animals and people on their premises, Mallard ducks can avoid such unpleasant situations as imprinting on a non-Mallard species like yourself. You will only be able to successfully raise birds as pugnacious as Mallard ducks by being attuned to changes in their behaviour and well-being.

Bringing home Mallard ducks will also lead to the eventuality hatchlings being born on your premises. These younger members will require special care and attention, either with their mothers or away under your care, based on your choices. Understand that improper care will surely result in your hatchlings falling ill, possibly even dying prematurely.

It is important that you carefully consider the option of gifting a mallard duck to another person, as they may not be equipped to handle the responsibilities that your entrust with a simple purchase. Whatever be your reasons for ultimately buying a Mallard duck, make sure they are made out of sensitivity and consideration towards your new potential companion.

Through this book, you will gain deeper insight in to the world of Mallard ducks - from their natural settings, to their behavioural patterns. You will also be guided through every stage of owning a Mallard duck, from initial thought to eventual rising. With a positive attitude and a dedicated spirit, you can work past the challenges that come with housing a Mallard duck and integrate them seamlessly into your life.

Chapter Two: Know your Mallard Duck

The Relationship between Mallard Ducks and Humans

It can be tricky to track down our first interaction with Mallard ducks; there is vague documentation recording the event. The first pieces of detailed information on these ducks can be found in Systema Naturae written by Carl Linnaeus in the 18th century. Compiled with information on many other species of birds, it is here that the Mallard duck is identified by its name.

The derivation of the name for Mallard ducks gives us an important clue not only about our relationship with the ducks, but about the defining role of language in history. The word Mallard is thought to be derived from the French word "*mallart*" or "*malart*" meaning wild drake.

Although the origins of this label are unknown, it is clear that the beloved Mallard has come a long way since its "wild" days. What's interesting to note is that this name can also be traced to *Madelhart*, a common name for German males at the time. The English language may have also contributed to the name of this duck with words such as "*mawdelard*" and "*maudelard*" used as adjectives around the time.

The debate around their nomenclature and discovery aside, these birds must have played a significant part of in the daily lives of people, being the ancestors of most domesticated ducks today.

Apart from their domestic value, it is their physical beauty that clearly captivated our imaginations even before the 18th century. The colorful Mallard duck made some of its earliest appearances in famed manuscripts such as the Sherborn Missal as early as the 15th century. Several illustrations decorating the margins of this text contain detailed depictions of the duck's vibrant plumage.

A common and popular species of duck in North America, the Mallard duck also embedded itself as part of the local culture. From appearances on heritage logos to their involvement in local traditions, the bond between the people of North America and Mallard ducks have been widely celebrated. A trip to the Peabody Hotel in Tennessee is a good example of this.

An intrinsic part of the surroundings, the Peabody Hotel has maintained four Mallard hens and a drake in their vicinity since 1933. Raised by local farmers under the best conditions, most Mallard ducks get to enjoy the Guest of Honour status at this hotel for a period of three months.

Every flock is returned to their cosy homes after this period, to make way for other esteemed "guests".

Our fascination with these ducks has prompted works of literature such as "Make way for the Ducklings", an illustrated story about Mallard duck parents-to-be. and Mallard ducks are also synonymous with the clothing brand Duck Head, appearing on their brand logo.   The Mallard Duck is also part of popular children's stories. The illustrated book "Make way for the Ducklings" was a very popular book that revolved around two Mallard Ducks who wanted to raise a family of their own.

It is through recordings such as illustrations, works of fiction and trade logos that we understand the impact of the Mallard duck on human history. With the enviable status of being one of the oldest domesticated duck breeds, it is no wonder, then, that the Mallard duck has left a subtle yet significant impact in our lives.

Natural Habitat

The ability to adapt with ease to a variety of conditions is probably why Mallard ducks are arguably the oldest of all domesticated duck species, second only to the Muscovies. This resilience to accept a diverse range of climate conditions, food and terrains has helped Mallard ducks thrive in both the Northern as well as the Southern Hemispheres. So great and strong is their geographical spread, that many regions measure the waterfowl health in their region using Mallard ducks as reference points.

In the Americas, you're most likely to find Mallard ducks in abundance From Central Alaska all the way down to Mexico. This part of the world houses so many Mallard ducks, that their population in North America crossed a cool 8.5 million in 2007. The Hawaiian Islands, though located a considerable distance away from the United States, also boasts of a healthy Mallard duck population of its own.

Across the ocean, Mallard ducks continue to comfortably inhabit the vast expanse of the Eurasian region. In the northern Hemisphere, expect to see lots of Mallard ducks in the Scandinavian region. As we move eastwards, Mallard ducks once again become abundant in East Asia, in Japan and China

Mallard ducks have also shown a fondness for the mildly tropical climates of the North African region; Morocco boasts of a large population of these ducks. And further still, Mallard ducks have made their homes in the southern regions of Australia and New Zealand.

Living conditions

It seems fairly clear by now that Mallard ducks will find a way to adapt to nearly any variation that location, climate and food sources may throw at them. This doesn't mean that Mallard ducks don't have living preferences, simply that they are not particularly fussy.

Even though Mallard ducks inhabit a wide variety of spaces, it is the wetlands that they most prefer. Salt or fresh water does not seem to matter - where there is water, the Mallard duck will find means to feed and reproduce. This species is most comfortable around water bodies such as lakes, rivers, estuaries and other smaller water bodies. The comfort that small lakes provide could be a reason why Mallard ducks are a popular fixture in public and private parks. However, Mallard ducks are at similar ease even along the shores of salt-water coasts.

Perhaps the only prerequisite that Mallard ducks look for before settling in is the depth of the surrounding water body. Their preferred settlements mostly comprise of waters that measure less than a meter. Aside from this one determining factor, as long as a location contains a sustainable food source, a water body and some level of privacy, you can expect a flock of Mallard birds to make it their home.

Mallard ducks and the ecology

Mallard ducks have managed to carve a unique existential zone within the ecology, thanks to their choice of habitat and feeding habits. Within the vast ecological space, Mallard ducks find themselves categorized with their medium-sized counterparts that live in semi-aquatic conditions. In addition, Mallard ducks further slot themselves into a niche by being semi-aquatic animals of medium-size who are also omnivorous in nature. The only other animals that exist as comfortably as Mallard ducks within these three parameters are aquatic turtles.

It may seem like sharing the same ecological space with aquatic turtles would bring out a natural competition to survive, as is part of ecological evolution. However, aquatic turtles and mallard ducks, have developed entirely distinct and separate strategies for survival, allowing them to co-exist within the same ecological spaces peacefully. Aquatic turtles have a lifespan of several decades, with the process of maturation spread out evenly through this time. Turtles are also very responsible reproducers, laying thousands of eggs over the course of their lives.

In comparison, our Mallard duck friends are considered extremely lucky to survive even a single decade. Due to a shorter life span, Mallard ducks attain complete maturity within their first year, spending the rest of their adult lives foraging for food and aiding in reproduction. And yet, while Mallard ducks may have superior reproduction abilities to many other aviary counterparts, they are certainly no match for the aquatic turtle's mission to produce as many young as it can. It is these varying life cycles that allow Mallard ducks and aquatic turtles to occupy the same spaces in the ecosystem without posing a threat to each other's existence.

As is the law of nature, Mallard ducks, like all other living beings, play several direct and indirect roles to help maintain ecological balance. One of their most significant roles is perhaps their contribution towards seed dispersal. Taken in through their feed and shed through their droppings, the Mallard ducks' preference for water bodies allows the seeds in their droppings to travel along water banks and plant themselves across a wider area. The ducks also allow for seeds dispersal through droppings when in flight.

It is not only the spread of seeds, but also the control of unwanted plants that Mallard ducks can claim responsibility for. Their fondness for pecking on wild grasses and weeds in their surroundings helps healthy plants thrive without any competition for food and light sources.

Mallard ducks also carry out this balancing act in the insect kingdom. By feeding on a steady supply of a variety of insects, this breed of ducks helps to maintain a regulated number of insects in an ecosystem. In fact, many personal accounts of Mallard duck post-mortem dissections have claimed their throats to be filled with insects of the winged variety - mosquitoes, flies, beetles etc.

The medium-sized bodies of the Mallard ducks help them escape the eyes of a number of predators along the food chain. They still, however, are an easy enough feeding target for such land animals as domestic and wild dogs, along with foxes or coyotes present in the same areas. While there have been observations of canine predators chasing adult ducks for food, coyotes, foxes and dogs have largely shown a preference for the easier-to-acquire eggs and hatchlings.

This doesn't mean that adult Mallard ducks are safe from the eyes of predators; aviary and aquatic predators have shown special fondness for adult Mallard ducks. This makes them obvious targets for such birds of prey as hawks, falcons and eagles, and even others, likes magpies and crows. But the Mallard ducks' preference for very shallow waters can be be explained as a means to avoid predators that lurk in slightly deep to very deep waters, such as crocodiles, snakes, otters, turtles and fish.

Apart from these naturally selected predators, Mallard ducks now also have human beings to contend with. An increasingly popular form of poultry in many parts of the world, the use of Mallard ducks as a food source could be an explanation for their depleting number in certain areas such as Mexico.

Chapter Three: Understand your Mallard Duck

1. Physical Traits and Appearance

Arguably one of the most beautiful of their family, Mallard ducks (*AnasPlatyrhynchos*) are classified as dabbling ducks belonging to the anatidae waterfowl group. While being categorized as medium-sized birds, Mallards ducks are noticeably larger than other dabbling ducks in the same category. This difference in size is a great example of Bergman's Rule, which observes that polar birds are comparatively larger than their tropical counterparts.

An adult Mallard duck usually grows to a length between 50 to 65cms, settling in at a weight in the range of 0.72 and 1.6 kilos. This weight makes them not only slightly larger, but also heavier than other dabbling ducks.

Another characteristic rule that Mallard ducks exhibit is Allen's Rule, which observes that polar birds develop noticeably smaller appendages in comparison to their tropical cousins as a means of minimizing heat loss. The ducks adhere to this rule with a modest wingspan measuring between 81 and 98cms.

A healthy adult Mallard duck is often classified by the above optimum length, weight and wingspan, along with three other important physical traits. The length of the wing chord is a crucial indicator, with a healthy measurement falling between 25.7 and 30.6cms. A bill that measures a minimum of 4.4cms is another indicator of good health while a tarsus measuring between 4 and 4.8cms confirms a Mallard duck to be of the highest quality.

Mallard ducks have an average life expectancy of around 3 years, with some domesticated Mallard ducks living slightly longer. As part of this considerably short lifespan, Mallard ducks develop fairly quickly, reaching full maturation and adulthood by the age of 14 months.

a.   Mallard ducklings

Mallard ducklings, when they hatch are usually black in colour, with speckles of yellow around their face and stomachs. The ducklings will also have a dark bill marked with a long bold stripe originating from the back of their eye. The darker colouring continues down their body, with jet-black feet. Younger Mallard ducks are also much plainer in appearance when compared to the older members, with dull and shabby coats and almost no white feathers.

As the ducklings age and mature, they develop further coats of colour based on their sex. It is interesting to note that the feathers of a duck become progressively unattractive in appearance before fully developing into a beautiful plumage. In the first two months, the black appearance of the duckling gives way to feathers and feet with a grey appearance. This colouring also signifies the passage of a duckling from a hatchling to a juvenile member.

It is between the third and fourth month that a Mallard duck's feathers and body coat take on their adult appearance. It is also during this time that the Mallard duck's wings develop for flight and its sex becomes apparent.

Interestingly, as the Mallard duck settles into adulthood, the drakes develop a distinctive colourful plumage with curved tails, while the feathers and coating of the females retain their duller appearance with straight tails. You will also notice shades of red around the drakes' chests, while the female chests remain brown. Another characteristic difference between the two genders includes the colour of the bill, which is yellow in males, and black and orange in females.

As the birds enter their adulthood, they become distinct in their colour. This is when the males will develop the characteristic plumage colours while the females remain almost the same. You will notice a change in the plumage when these birds transition between the breeding periods. This is usually at the onset and after the moulting period.

While they may have many differences, the plumage of Mallard drakes and ducks do share one similarity - the colour of their speculum patches. Present on the wing, these deep blue-purple feathers are most visible when the ducks are flying, and make for an arresting sight. Usually shed in the summer months, Mallard ducks will grow back these beautiful feathers almost immediately after they fall off.

b.   Male Mallard ducks

A male Mallard duck that has attained full maturity is extremely easy to spot, thanks to their distinctly colored coat. These male specimen are distinguished by a shiny bottle-green head with a white collar-like marking around the neck separating the head from the body. A healthy male adult Mallard duck will also have a brightly-colored orange bill punctuated with a jet-black tip.

The chest of a Mallard duck bursts into a startling deep purple shade, before settling into a pale grey around the belly. The wingspan of the Mallard duck may carry some of this grey merged with shades of brown.

It is, however, the tail of the Mallard duck that is considered its most attractive feature. Among the various shades of green, orange, purple, grey, and brown, it is the jet-black of the Mallard duck's tail that stands out.

c.   Female Mallard ducks

Female Mallard ducks are often less attractive to look at than their male counterparts, but are beautiful nonetheless. Upon attaining maturity, female ducks develop a plumage that consists of varying shades of brown.

While the neck and throat areas of the female duck are a pale, almost ashen brown in colour, the regions around the eyes and crown are significantly darker. The bodies of females Mallard ducks bear great resemblance to other dabbling ducks in their group. This appearance is characterized by a speckled and mottled coating in contrasting shades of brown and white. Individualistic in appearance, every female duck will have a different and distinct colouring on her body.

Due to their similarity to other dabbling ducks, it is often easy to confuse Mallard female ducks with other breeds. Most commonly, Mallard ducks are mistaken for such ducks as the Gadwall, although close inspection will show you the differences between the two. Noticeably, Female Gadwall and Mallard ducks have similar looking bills as well as stomachs, in terms of colouring.

If you have spent time with Mallard ducks, however, you will notice obvious difference in the shading between the two breeds. This is also true for the American Black duck, another breed that the female Mallard is often confused with.

Mallard ducks in captivity may differ in colour from those in the wild, although this often signals breeding with hybrids. Pure-bred Mallard ducks will almost always exhibit the above signs of colouring. In recent times, however, breeders have been taking greater interest in breeding Mallard ducks with varying plumage.

Here are some of duck breeds most commonly confused with the adult Mallard duck:

Name	Resemblance	Differences
American Black Duck	Male or female adult mallard during eclipse stage	Darker plumage, darker tail, distinct black-bordered blue patch on the wing
Mottled Duck	Male or female adult mallard during eclipse stage	Paler face, darker tail, unmarked throat

Gadwall	Female Adult Mallard	Mildly misshapen two-toned head, brown and silver colorings on body and wings, two-toned bill and white patch on wing in female Gadwalls, :
Northern Shoveler	Male Adult Mallard	Distinct blue patch on wing, white chest with brown coloring, broad spatula-like bill
Red Breasted Merganser	Male Adult Mallard	Bold white collar, white and grey stripes on the sides and back, serrated bill, shaggy coated chest

2. Mallard ducks and the Reproductive Cycle

Due to the societal nature of Mallard ducks, females will select a drake most desirable to them when they are ready to mate. This selected drake will usually be the biggest in physical size, may have the most impressive plumage and crest, and may also be the most aggressive of the flock. It is such dominant behaviour that makes a Mallard drake attractive to sexually active females.

What is interesting to note, however, is that Mallard ducks do not mate with just one female, as other members of the duck family do. Staying true to their reputation of being prolific breeders, Mallard drakes will impregnate multiple female over the course of their lives. Those Mallard drakes within the flock that are deemed unfit for mating, usually congregate to form their own sub-groups - a flock of bachelors, if you will.

The timing of sexual activity among Mallard ducks greatly depends on their geographical locations and climatic conditions. Most comfortable in warm and moist conditions, Mallard ducks will reproduce during the summer months of the hemisphere they are located in. Therefore, the breeding season for ducks in the northern half will last between March and September, while those in the southern parts will breed between August and May.

Another trait that sets Mallards apart from their duck cousins is their willingness to copulate on any surface. While most duck species prefer the privacy that water provides, Mallards are just at ease copulating on land as well, perhaps another sign of their dominant natures.

The act of impregnation itself is carried out when the drake inserts his spirally-shaped penis into the similarly-shaped vagina of a female. This unique shape of the ducks genitalia spiral in different direction in the drake and the female. According to many behaviourists and waterfowl experts, these opposing shapes could be a natural defence mechanism that protects females against forceful impregnation by aggressive drakes.

Once a Mallard drake and duck have successfully mated, the female sets out to prepare a comfortable brooding spot. Female Mallards prefer hidden nesting spots that are difficult to access, such as hollows in tree barks raised up to 20 metres above the ground. Areas with thick vegetative growth and low visibility are also preferred, as they provide protection against unwanted predators.

Domesticated Mallard females will replicate the art of nest building by gathering soft materials available in their premises and setting it up in preferred corners. Once the nest is ready, the females lay an egg daily, till she has collected a batch of up to 16 eggs. Upon reaching her desired number, the female duck stops laying further eggs and perches herself on the batch, providing warmth and incubation till the eggs hatch.

Duck eggs only begin the process of development and hatching when they receive the first bout of incubation; the female will avoid providing this warmth till she has laid her last egg. This act is the female duck's way of timing the birth of her hatchlings, which makes feeding and resting easier for the mother and the ducklings as well.

During the brooding period, female Mallard ducks will leave their spots unattended for only an hour or so a day. They use this time to perform their daily ablutions, and maybe exercise their wings and feet. The eggs of Mallard ducks living in the wild or raised in open housing environment are most susceptible to predatory attacks during this time.

Provided the female Mallard can safely incubate her eggs for an extended period, hatchlings will emerge from the eggs after about 35 days. This hatching period is curiously longer by a week, when compared to other ducks. The duckling first emerges by forming a tiny hole or "pip" in the shell. Chipping away at the eggshell will an especially formed calcified tip, ducklings will successfully break out of their shell after about 24 hours from the first crack.

While slightly wet as soon as they burst from their shells, ducklings will dry off fairly quickly, and will open their eyes almost instantly. Within a few hours, most hatchling will have dried off completely, and begun to walk about unsteadily.

For the first few weeks, young hatchlings cannot provide enough warmth and sustenance for themselves, and are tended to by their mother. Over the course of these formative weeks, the mother also takes up the responsibility of introducing such concepts as foraging, feeding, drinking and bathing to her young ones.

The reproductive cycle is then carried forward when the ducklings mature into an adult flock and begin sexual activity during the nearest mating season.

It is also interesting to note that while the Mallard drakes are highly involved in the earlier stages of mating, they seldom participate in the construction of nests of the subsequent care that ducklings require. These roles are generally limited to the female members of the flock alone.

3. Mallard ducks and the gender change phenomenon

Mallard ducks are very fascinating birds with a number of unique traits and phenomena to their credit; among these is the widely-observed phenomena that Mallard ducks can and may change their genders at some stage in their lives. While this change has not been consistent, and there has been no specific explanation discovered for this occurrence, the gender change phenomenon has been observed among some Mallard ducks.

Two possible theories have been suggested as explain this mystifying gender reversal process. The first is a biological theory that observes a quirk in the female Mallard's ovaries. Of the pair, one ovary is usually benign and produces a significant amount of testosterone that contributes to the physical plumage of the duck. Experts believe that an incomplete or improper transition during puberty may cause the duck to exhibit male physical traits, while having no impact on the egg-laying abilities of the duck.

Another explanation points to the particularly aggressive nature of the adult Mallard flock. Behaviourists suggest the mating season can be highly traumatic for many Mallard females due to the competitive natures of the drakes. In order to avoid injury or forceful impregnation by the males, some females may react by exhibiting male traits that disguise their reproductive abilities. While it may sound far-fetched, this theory has been backed by many a breeder and owner who has noticed significant behavioural and sexual changes in Mallard females.

While the exact cause behind the gender change phenomenon is still undetermined, it is certain that this change occurs only in the secondary sexual traits, into the primary ones. This means that your Mallard duck may suddenly display the physical and behavioural traits of a drake, but can certainly not impregnate any other ducks, as she is ultimately, still a female duck.

Chapter Four: The Mallard Duck as a Pet

It is easy to become charmed by the Mallard duck; their colourful plumage and quirky personalities are attractive to many people. Popular culture and the calm demeanour of ducks also makes it seem like the Mallard duck would be a low-maintenance pet to have around. You should understand that Mallard ducks require specific living conditions to thrive, and these conditions have to successfully merge with your already existing environment. Before you bring home a Mallard duck therefore, you have a few concepts to consider:

Mallard ducks are a lifelong commitment

Mallard ducks are highly intelligent, loyal and productive to have around as pets, but they are also among the most demanding. Many Mallard duck owner and breeders will narrate tales of how the distinctive personalities of Mallard ducks can make them challenging companions, if rewarding in the long term.

From the day you decide to bring home a Mallard duck, you make a series of choices that require dedication to undertake and maintain. You will have to ensure that your ducks are raised in a hygienic setting that is constantly replenished with food, water and space to explore.

You will have to be committed towards finding the best food sources, since Mallard ducks are susceptible to illness from stale or badly prepared food. Mallard ducks also require secure spaces to retreat to each night, and you have to be dedicated towards keeping these pens as clean as possible.

Young hatchlings require constant monitoring and guidance till they reach maturity, and once they are adults, you have to pay special attention to the egg-laying females. If you choose to breed your ducks for their eggs, this decision then requires additional responsibilities and decision.

All your Mallard ducks will need to be taught the appropriate spots to food, forage and bathe. Teaching them such skills as herding requires time and patience. When your ducks are let out for the day, you have to be committed towards ensuring their safety against predators and injury.

It is not only the ducks themselves that need your constant care and attention; Mallard ducks interact directly with their surroundings, and you are now responsible to maintain a balance in this environment. You have to account for the vegetation and insect life consumed by your Mallard and provides an ecologically safe space for your ducks to inhabit.

In the eight or so years of their lives, Mallard ducks may become highly susceptible to infections or injuries, and will also require constant health examinations. For this purpose, you will have to first find, and then maintain a good relationship with a qualified waterfowl expert and veterinarian in your area.

This exhaustive list of prerequisites is enough to make any interested duck owner reconsider their decisions, but with some dedication and a fixed routine in place, you can make Mallard ducks a part of your life and family.

Adult Mallards or ducklings - whom should you bring home?

When you decide to bring home a Mallard duck, you should also take the time to consider the preferred age of your soon-to-be family members. Many potential duck owners often find themselves conflicted between the choice to bring home fully-grown adult Mallards or raise baby hatchlings into adults. Your ultimate decision should be one that addresses the purposes behind bring home Mallard ducks.

The first issue that you should address is the purpose of the new Mallard duck in your household - are they your first duck, or are they brought to add to an already existing flock? If this is your first experience with handling and caring for Mallard ducks, it may be preferable to bring home young hatchlings.

Mallard ducks are impressionable, and are also creatures of routine and habit. By bringing home a young one, you make it easier for the duck to embrace you as a caregiver. You also receive the joy of watching your duck or ducks develop into beautiful, proud birds. Hatchlings are also relatively easy and cheap to buy, and can be found with nearly all local vendors and breeders.

Young hatchlings are easy to train and mould - you will have little to no problems helping them developing such habits as herding and foraging. If you can raise hatchlings in a stable and calm environment, you can also control how temperamental your ducks will grow up to be. Mallard ducklings also tend to be friendlier and more approachable towards other animals than their adult counterparts, and so make a healthy addition to a mixed-animal setting.

But perhaps the biggest advantage that comes with bringing home a Mallard hatchling is their hygienic and healthy condition. Young hatchlings are less likely to have transmitted infectious bacteria, and you can ensure that they are raised in the best conditions.

If you already have your own community of ducks at home, however, hatchlings may not easily blend into an already evolved environment. An adult community of ducks requires an adult Mallard to properly adapt to the aggressive initiation ritual that is establishing a new pecking order. While your society of ducks may shun and even bully younger ducklings, they are more likely to treat an adult Mallard with acceptance.

The true advantage in bringing home an adult Mallard lies in the productive value they can have for you. Based on your needs, you can bring home an adult female Mallard to supply eggs for hatching or consumption. If a thriving and productive duck community is your goal, you can bring home a flock of drakes and female ducks, without having to wait for them to pass their formative years. Many duck breeders and hobbyists also like to bring home rare species of adult Mallards for exhibition purposes.

Bringing home an adult Mallard is also a wise choice if you are adopting a Mallard duck from a nearby shelter. By providing medical attention and care to a traumatized adult Mallard, you form a closer bond with your adopted duck.
No matter what the age of the duck you ultimately do bring home, it is essential that the animal be in as healthy a state as possible. Have your duck checked for any existing medical conditions, and give it an initial period in quarantine, till they adapt to their surroundings.

Mallard Ducks and common "quack" tales

Mallard ducks are such an intrinsic part of our daily surroundings that folklore and local superstition has caused us to confuse our Mallard ducks facts with fiction. Indeed, many duck owners will reveal believing for at least one of the following commonly believed myths about Mallard ducks. It is important to remember that the life, health and behaviour of Mallard ducks depends greatly on the living conditions that you provide; trust your waterfowl experts and refrain from believing any of the following stories:

Myth	Fact
Mallard ducks are aggressive and hostile.	Aggression is part of the Mallard duck's nature, but is more commonly exhibited only by the drakes. This behaviour, if observed, should signal that the drake is in the middle of the breeding season and considers you to be a threat or competition. During the non-mating months, you will often find that Mallard ducks are agreeable, even mildly friendly birds to interact with.
Mallard ducks make you instantly rich	Mallard ducks are profitable to their owners - they provide them with a constant supply of eggs and subsequent hatchlings for personal use. this process, however, takes time, patience, financial capital and a large number of Mallard ducks. It is foolish to expect overnight success with just pair of ducks and around 200 eggs a year to sell and use.
Mallard ducks can be kept indoors like other animals	All ducks require open space to forage, feed and rest; keeping them in your surroundings may be too stressful for the birds. Additionally, ducks are messy creatures are easy carriers for

	such sickness as Salmonella. To avoid ailments from spreading to you or your family members, ensure that your ducks are housed in a safe location away from your living space.
Touching the skin of a Mallard duck will give you warts	The skin of a Mallard duck does have a unique feel to it. IT is rubbery, almost leathery in texture, besides having a slightly abrasive surface. This skin, however, is not infectious and will not give you warts. The duck's skin, however, is still an open environment for harmful bacteria to nest on, so it is best to clean you hands after every interaction with your ducks.
Mallard ducks will not leave if you provide lots of food	The only way to physically prevent your Mallard duck from flying away is by pinning or clipping away their wings and feathers, although these practices are frowned upon by many. Mallard ducks, however, prefer comfortable settings and are unlikely to leave a setting that has ample food, water and shelter. Most Mallard duck owners come to accept the possibility that their birds may become dissatisfied and choose to leave for various reasons.
If you breed differently colored ducks, the duckling will	The process of breeding and mutation is a complex one that is determined by a variety of genetic factors and interactions. While you may achieve

display a mix of their colours	the desired state of colouring in your duckling, simply breeding differently colored ducks cannot ensure a consistent result each time.
A healthy-looking Mallard duck is also internally healthy	This is probably the most dangerous myth that human tend to believe about poultry, especially ducks. Mallard ducks are resilient to many types of bacteria and viruses that infect other forms of life. Additionally, they may also be carriers for the symptoms of such diseases, while not displaying any outward signs of having the disease. A good example of such a sickness is salmonella. This is why you should ensure that your Mallard duck receives constant medical examination by an experienced waterfowl expert.

Chapter Five: Selecting your Mallard Ducks

Once you have put careful thought into the consequences that bringing home a Mallard duck can have, it is best to find the right sources to purchase your duck from. Buying a mallard duck takes more effort than walking into a shop and selecting the cutest duck. a variety of factors determine whether the Mallard on offer is in good enough condition to take home with you.

When you set out to buy a Mallard duck, aim to return with the healthiest ducks of the bunch. You can only receive a complete bill of health from your local waterfowl expert, but a few simple physical indicators should reveal the condition of your prospective duck:

1.   The eyes of the duck should be clear, and not clouded over, sunken or oozing any liquids,

2.   A healthy Mallard Duckling can walk almost immediately after they hatch. Any duckling that is lethargic or immobile is unhealthy,

3.   The duck should either be flapping its wings or have them resting flatly against its body. Any irregular positioning of the wing signals injury, even deformity,

4.   Healthy Mallard ducks will be social and active among their member, even in a closed setting,

5.   A healthy Mallard Duck will constantly look for food sources; lack of appetite is an indicator of poor health,

6.   While Mallard ducks are messy, they are not unhygienic. If the prospective duck is covered in his own faecal matter, which is alarmingly smelly, the duck is not healthy.

7.   Finally, check the duck for visible injuries, scars, sores or wounds. Only if the duck can clear all your health inspection should you ask the vendors for the price.

The Price of Mallard Ducks

How much you pay to bring home your Mallard ducks will vary on a number of deciding factors - the source that you buy the duck from, the number of ducks you decide to buy, the age of the ducks at the time of purchase, their physical appearance and plumage, just to name a few. Furthermore, an always-fluctuating market for the purchase of animals makes it difficult to pin down a uniform price on the Mallard ducks of your choice.

Despite minor differences in the prices, you will generally be able to acquire Mallard hatchlings with common colour coats for anywhere between £2 to £18 per duckling. The prices may then increase for hatchlings with rare colour coats, adult Mallards, and so on. Do not be too surprised if your vendor quotes an unreasonable amount for a rare

Mallard in their shops - there have been records of a Mallard drake auctioned off for £1,500 in 2012!

The price of Mallard ducks cannot only be limited to calculating their individual costs. You also have to account for their housing initial housing expenses,, feeding and bathing supplies, as well as health requirements. Depending on the scale of your endeavour, these costs may range from a few hundred pounds to tens of thousands.

You may find that you can cut down on some expenses, such as providing a specialized swimming space, by using an old kid's pool for your ducks. You can also use old containers for nesting, vessels for feeding, and construction materials form around your premises. When it comes to the feed and medical supplies, however, avoid finding cheaper alternatives and select only the best options for your ducks.

Social Considerations

Whether you ultimately bring home a mallard duckling or an adult, you should also make considerations for the social environment that your ducks will be raised in. While it is understood that you are the primary caregiver, Mallard ducks are still social creatures that need to mingle with their own kind to develop in a healthy manner.

Bearing this trait in mind, you should try to avoid bringing home a single Mallard, young or adult, male or female. In the absence of a similar role model, ducks will adopt the next available species as their parental figure, which may become confusing for them when it is time to mate and socialize.

This unique concept of imprinting may also prevent your duck from embracing any new members, should you add them to the pen at a later stage. Mallard ducks tend to adapt best with those members they see from their early days; try and foster such a social setting for all your ducks.

Many breeders and experts advise that new owners begin with a group of three or four Mallard ducks - one drake and the rest egg-laying females. Now that the members of your group are determined, ensure that you pick the right genders from your breeder or vendor. If you are bringing home members younger than seven weeks, you may not be able to tell the drakes and ducks apart.

Ask your breeder or expert for guidance in this matter, and if there are unsure, pick up older members whose genders are easily distinguishable. You can either bring home adults from a similar group or start a new community with specifically-selected Mallards; a tight-knit community among your ducks will form only with your sensitive approach towards the ducks.

Buying from Breeders

When you do your research to find reliable sources to purchase Mallard ducks, most suggestions will point you towards Mallard duck breeders, and with good reason. Mallard duck breeders are among the most passionate and enthusiastic caregivers you will find, and usually raise high-quality Mallards for sale.

Since this is a way of life for them, Mallard duck breeders will have hatchlings and adults ducks on sale all year round. You will also have the opportunity to better study various other breeds, as breeders often raise more than three or four species at a time.

Mallard duck breeders are very particular about such factors as the health of the ducks, the quality of their feed, their physical appearance and their overall temperament. Unlike many retail vendors, Mallard duck breeders raise their birds themselves, and can confidently guarantee you a duck of high breeding and good health.

Breeders are often the best people to contact when you need assistance in matters such as finding a waterfowl expert, receiving the right permits for housing, etc. Furthermore, breeders seldom charge exorbitant prices for their ducklings; most are happy to offer them at very reasonable rates. Should you find a suitable breeder in your area, try to forge a relationship with them. They may turn out to be your greatest allies in your endeavour to raise Mallard ducks.

Buying from Vendors

When you think of buying a new Mallard duck, your most obvious option may be the local pet retail store. It should be noted, however, that not all retail vendors will stock up on Mallard ducks, especially adults.

Ducks require a lot of attention and care that the vendors may not be able to provide. Larger vendors may have designated areas for birds, and may sometimes bring in a batch or two of hatchlings. You may find other ducks such as Peking and Gadwall more easily than the Mallard, but with some careful research, Mallard duck vendors should not be hard to track down.

When you do find a suitable Mallard duck vendor, you give yourself a number of buying advantages. Vendors can offer you a variety of Mallards, with differently colored plumage, and distinct personalities. This gives you the freedom to select a Mallard duck that you take a personal liking to.

An experienced duck vendor is also a reliable source for any information that you may need for your duck's welfare. They will usually have good waterfowl experts to recommend, and can also guide you towards finding the right housing and feeding supplies for your ducks. The more professional of these vendors also offer basic health benefits and care packages, so do enquire about these facilities.

You should bear in mind that such professional services will cost some money, definitely more than a breeder would charge you. Professional vendors, however, will not overcharge you for your ducks, especially if you are buying them in a group. The price may be only reasonably higher than that of the breeder, will ensure a trusted source for your purchase.

Buying from Individuals

While this may be the most uncommon of all your buying choices, Mallard duck hobbyists and owners will also give up hatchlings and even adults for sale. Any Mallard duck owners often find themselves with more hatchlings than they can take care of, thanks to the prolific egg-laying abilities of our female friends. If the number is too large for them to raise on their own, you will find advertisements posted by them on such public forums as newspapers, community message boards and online service websites.

Buying your Mallard ducks from enthusiasts and owners can often be your best choice, if you are able to track down such sellers. Experienced Mallard duck owners raise their animals in their best conditions and will mostly sell you healthy ducks at very reasonable rates.

Adopting a Mallard duck

In case you don't want to spend lots of money to purchase a Mallard duck, or cannot find a trusted source in your area to buy one from, you can choose to adopt a Mallard duck from a shelter closest to you.

Adoption is often a rewarding experience for the duck keeper, as well as the duck itself. By making this choice, you can bring home and nurture a pet of your own. Adopting a Mallard duck, however, can also be a tricky and delicate experience to navigate through.

When you find a Mallard duck that you'd like to adopt, ensure that you have it examined for any ailments, infections or other health conditions. Even if you do find a perfectly healthy Mallard duck, understand that it will need constant care through food, water and medical attention.

The duck may need even more nurturing if it has had a traumatic past in the wild or with a previous owner.

The choice to adopt a Mallard duck comes with its own set of responsibilities and duties, but if you have the commitment and patience to raise your Mallard duck, adopting your pet will be one of the best decisions you make.

Chapter Six: Housing your Mallard duck

Housing conditions for your Mallard ducks should and will be among your chief priorities when you decide to bring them home. Since Mallard ducks adapt easily to just about any surroundings, you will have great flexibility when determining the ideal housing space for them.

You may have the resources to provide your ducks with natural or artificial ponds, foraging areas, and maximum security against predators. Or you may prefer that your Mallard ducks roam freely in your backyard with little crates of water for feeding.

You may live in a cold area that requires additional heating to keep your ducks warm, or may live in a tropical area that will need cooling facilities. Do not fret over which housing condition is ideal for your ducks; there are plenty of options that come with their own benefits and drawbacks.

Mallard duck owners generally design housing spaces to blend the environmental conditions with the needs of their ducks. To be at their most comfortable, your ducks require cosy nesting spots, ample food and water sources, space to exercise their wings and feet, and some form of security against possible predators. So long as the above, and the following factors are considered, you can easily modify your surroundings to house your duck:

1. Adequate number of nooks, crannies and personal zones for all your ducks. These spaces are used by the ducks when they need "alone time", and are essential to maintain a calm environment.

2. Optimum temperatures within the spaces that help keep your ducks comfortable. While hatchlings require their heating conditions to be constantly monitored, adult Mallards can easily adapt to a pre-determined temperature, preferably around 55 degrees Fahrenheit.

3. The degree of security you want to provide to your Mallard ducks. Different housing options come with their own sets of drawbacks, especially in terms of protection against predators. In addition, the enclosure itself has to be free of unhygienic conditions or toxic growth.

4. The amount of freedom you want to give your Mallard ducks, for exploration as well as possible escape. Certain housing options are more effective than others at preventing your ducks from flying away. If you have opted against practices such as pinioning and feather clipping, you will have to decide how your housing space may prevent or encourage this act.

5. The accessibility of the housing areas to your own is also a crucial factor. While you don't want the ducks to be

located too far from your eye, their enclosures should also not crowd areas like picnic spots or play areas used by your children. The eventual aim of the Mallard ducks' enclosure is to merge seamlessly into your personal space.

Housing for Hatchlings

If you're bringing Mallard ducks into your home for the first time, you may be most comfortable adopting hatchlings instead of older ducks. These younger members will adapt to new surroundings with greater ease, and will also accept you as their caregiver.

Even if you plan on giving your Mallard ducks an open outdoor space to roam and forage, hatchlings are best housed in indoor conditions. This is your best bet to ensure their safety against predatory attacks in your absence. You should determine a spot that is a little away from your living quarters, but close enough that you can keep a timely watch on them. A spare tool shed, an unused garage or an empty log cabin in your vicinity make for ideal housing options.

As with any pets that are housed indoors, your hatchlings are likely to leave a smelly mess in their pens or cages; ensure that you keep the surroundings as odour-free and germ-free as possible, Cleaning their quarters at least once daily will help keep you and your ducks healthy. Apart from clean surroundings, strive to provide fresh food and water for your hatchlings at a fixed schedule.

Optional embellishments can include an extra source of water for swimming; your hatchlings will appreciate the early encouragement towards exercise. You can also place a heat lamp within their pens for a source of heat and warmth. While not essential, such features will help build a healthy, nurturing for environment your hatchlings.

The structure of the shelter itself does not need to be very sophisticated. Your hatchlings will be perfectly content in a makeshift housing spot erected by pinning some boards together, or even in a large wooden crate. Make the housing space comfortable for your hatchlings by covering the bottom with layers of soft material. Choose from such sources as straw, grass or thin strips of paper and cotton to provide a layer of cushioning against the cold floor.

Mallard ducklings and water

A water source for swimming is beneficial for your Mallard ducks' upbringing, but it is certainly not essential. Swimming is a way for your ducks to exercise their wings, but they can easily get this exercise on land as well. Furthermore, Mallard hatchlings don't begin swimming immediately, so you do not have to worry about providing them with a space to swim.

What they do require, however, is plenty of fresh water provided at constant intervals. The health of your hatchlings depends greatly on the quality of the water they drink. Lack of fresh, replenished water for drinking can sicken; even kill your hatchlings in under three days.

In your urge to provide lots of water for the hatchlings, however, avoid placing a bowl that is too deep. Young Mallard ducks aren't yet equipped for swimming but are curious - they may drown in a deep water bowl or container. A wide, shallow vessel made from such materials as plastic, glass or even ceramic are ideal.

You can also find specialized drinking apparatus with nipple dispensers that help young animals drink comfortably. If you choose these for the hatchlings, you will need to teach them how to drink from them.

Despite your best efforts, you will almost always find dirty water containers when you return to the pens. Ducklings can be messy and boisterous, and will splash the water out, while dirtying the bowls themselves. The only way to ensure your ducks have clean drinking water is to clean their vessels on a daily basis.

Around their third or fourth week, your Mallard ducklings will become increasingly active; this signals their readiness to begin swimming. You can introduce them to the activity by placing shallow vessels for them to navigate in. Find vessels with low rims and fill them with water that's about half an inch or less in depth. Such conditions are sufficient till your ducklings become confident, stronger swimmers.

Once your ducklings have reached the seven week mark, they're no longer dependent little members of your community; in fact, your ducks are now ready to move to more adult housing conditions. Your ducks, who are creatures of habit, have by now become accustomed to their cosy hatchling spaces. You, therefore, have to try and usher them into their adult surroundings without causing them stress.

The best ways to ease your ducks into their new homes is to introduce them to the new space in small bursts. Let them spend a few minutes in the new area for the first day, and gradually increase their time by a few minutes daily. Take this opportunity to practice herding your ducks as well.

Building an enclosure for adult Mallard ducks

Whether you are bringing home new adult Mallard ducks, or transitioning your ducklings into their new housing spaces, the ideal settings for your ducks are often the simplest ones. Mallard ducks, being highly adaptable, require only the bare necessities to settle down.

To ensure a stress-free environment for your adult ducks, select a spot in an open area of your premises and erect or attach a secure pen. You can also provide a makeshift source of water that allows your ducks to swim and exercise. Kid-size pools or large tubs are perfect additions to outdoor pens, and provide easy drainage and refilling options.

Materials best suited to construct your pen include wood and wire mesh for simpler structures, or cement for sturdier enclosures. While many duck owners find wood to be a strong enough barrier against harsh weather and predators, cement enclosures have become popular among those breeders who raise ducks in hazardous environments. Cement is also favourable as it provides an opaque cover for the ducks against the outside world, while being smooth enough that it doesn't cause tears and injuries on the ducks' bodies.

It does not matter if your enclosure does not have a floor; Mallard ducks are comfortable using the ground as their housing space. You can, however, create cosy nooks and corners for egg-laying females and other ducks. Your enclosures should also be spacious enough to allow constant air circulation; stale and stagnant air can make your ducks ill. A housing space with an area of 100 square feet makes for an ideal setting in which to house a pair of adult Mallards.

Raised Pens

Enclosed pens are perfect spaces for your Mallard ducks to retreat in; but having a pen erected directly on the ground also makes for extra cleaning for you. With some simple construction work, you can easily raise the pen off the floor. This may take some work and preparation, but will be a convenient option for you in the long term.

A raised pen is often designed the same way as a regular pen is - with materials such as wood designed in a crate-like fashion. Wooden flooring for the pen allows the excrement to slide through the cracks to the ground. You will also design the frame to be slightly elevated from the ground, with the sides covered with protective material such as wire mesh.

The main advantage behind having an elevated enclosure is the promise of a cleaner and healthier environment for your ducks. Any mess in the form of food, water or droppings will slip through the enclosure and can be cleaned off the ground without upsetting your ducks.

An elevated enclosure also allows you to design a simple drainage system for your ducks' swimming areas. All you will need to do is find an old unused kid-size pool and make a hole to fit your drainage pipe through. Use this pipe to both fill and empty the pool, when not in use by the ducks. Water that is drained out can be used for the plants in your garden or backyard. Instead of dealing with stagnant and stale water that accumulates in the water enclosures, this drainage system gives elevated enclosures an edge over their floored counterparts.

As comfortable as elevated enclosures will be, you will need to make them comfortable for the ducks by covering the sides of the pen. These covers will shield your Mallard ducks predators, harsh weather conditions, and abrupt changes in their surroundings. You can provide an easy cover for your ducks by mounting your pen against a wall, and covering the other three sides.

If you live in cold areas, an open floor may allow windy drafts to seep through the cracks and chill your ducks. You can avoid this by either placing heating pans on the floor, or placing a layer of covering under the porous floor.

Apart from the convenience it provides, elevated pens are ultimately attractive because they protect your ducks from predatory attacks. Wild animals and birds of prey are highly unlikely to break into a secure pen, especially one that provides the obstacle of being raised off the ground.
It is for this assurance of security that raised pens are a preferred form of housing for hatchlings and younger Mallard ducks. The younger members do not need vast expanses of land to wander on; a pen that has about 100 square feet of space within and a height of 100 centimetres is ideal for a batch of little ducklings.

The only other preparation you will need to make before erecting raised pens is acquiring the necessary permits from your local authorities. Some areas, especially urban residential spaces, prefer to be informed when a group of birds are housed among the community. Once you receive the green signal from the required offices, you can implement and reap the long-term benefits of elevated pens.

Free Range

Plenty of open space to explore and forage is one of the Mallard duck's prime requisites for ideal housing, and the free-range option of housing is one that most adheres to your ducks' wishes. This setting may not be easy to come by - you'd require a considerable portion of open land at your disposal. If you do own some land, however, you should certainly consider this housing option.

Allowing your ducks to wander about on open land closely imitates their natural settings, making them comfortable. Free space to forage, nest and socialize greatly contributes towards the general well-being of your ducks.

In order to let your ducks roam about freely, however, you will have to ensure that your land is properly protected against predatory attacks. Depending on the predators in your area, protection can vary from erecting a simple fence around your perimeter, to setting up alarms and traps outside your area.

Your Mallard ducks will appreciate an open setting to wander in, but this setting also makes them vulnerable to attacks not only from animals on land, but birds of prey as well. Birds such as hawks and falcons find younger ducks easy to hunt, but will keep away if there is a larger animal to guard the flock, such as a guard dog.

You may feel like the free-range option requires extra work and dedication on your part - this is definitely true. The choice to go free-range is usually taken only by those who are dedicated to providing a setting that mirrors the ducks' natural environment.

It takes a great deal of responsibility to make the ducks as comfortable as possible, while protecting them from attacks and providing them with constant food and water sources.

Furthermore, Mallard ducks are noisy and messy creatures, who will leave their mark in your immediate surroundings. It is important that the members of your community are open to having a flock of ducks in their setting. Your duck may happily wander into someone else's yard, pluck at their plants and flowers, may be hunted by other domestic animals, or may become agitated and charge at a friendly neighbour.

Many owners who choose the free-range option may already have favourable conditions on their premises, such as a pond or a water stream for the ducks to swim in, a tranquil setting away from neighbours or chicken coops that have free space for housing.

Nearly all free-range duck owner also refrain from such practices as pinioning and feather clipping, out of respect for their animals. Once Mallard ducks find that their settings provide them with adequate food, water, security and space to roam, they tend to settle, instead of flying away. If you share similar conditions, or can provide a relaxed environment for your ducks, the free-range method of housing may just be the one for you.

Herding

While free-range housing certainly gives your ducks freedom of movement, they will still require closed, secure spaces for nesting, feeding and sleeping. In their natural setting, these nooks and crannies give Mallard ducks safety from abrupt weather changes and predators, along with a place to brood and nest. Not all open land will have large trees with secure hollows or safe enclosures created by naturally placed rocks, however. In such instances, duck breeders blend the freedom of free-range housing with the security of enclosed housing.

It is not difficult to set up safe enclosures for your ducks on open land. Simply select a quiet corner on your land to construct simple pens or housing spaces for your ducks, big enough to accommodate the flock comfortably at night. If you already have an empty garage, tool-shed or unused log cabin, all you have to do is set up the interiors to make your ducks comfortable.

You responsibility does not simply end at building these safe zones for your ducks. Your flock will also need to be taught to retreat to this space every night, and to leave the space when the sun rises. It may take some a few days or weeks to train all your ducks, but herding is a rewarding practice in the long run. Providing your ducks with distinct areas for rest and activity will contribute to their well-being, and by learning to shed droppings outside during the day, will also help keep their housing spaces cleaner.

With a little practice in the technique of herding, discussed in a later chapter, you can rest assured that your ducks will always have some protection from threats, even in the free-range housing method.

Constructing a Pond for your Mallard ducks

We have already discussed how ponds are favourable, but not integral to the survival of your Mallard ducks. You do not need a pond, lake or stream in order to bring home some ducks. However, if you want to provide a water source such as a pond for the flock, it is possible to have one constructed by yourself.

To construct your own pond, you have a list of prerequisites that need to be fulfilled. The first of them is doing your homework to ensure that you can construct a pond on your land. Take the time to research all the permits and licenses you may require to erect your own water supply source in the area - different regions have different laws governing the use of land.

You should also speak to the local land and resource experts in the area to determine how beneficial a pond can be in your surroundings. Constructing a source that hold water for long periods of time needs the right kinds of soil, watershed abilities and irrigation facilities. Your selected land should also be able to withstand conditions such as flooding without causing damage to your property or to the ones around you.

Once you do determine how suitable your land is, you then have to pick a spot to construct your pond on. Ideal spaces are spots low to the ground with gently raised edges that allow water to collect. You can take advantages of this spot by digging out the mud and using it to secure the raised edges for your pond.

At the outset, you should understand that pond construction is a costly affair; this procedure will add a few thousand dollars to your Mallard duck expenditures at the least. Once you do make this decision, however, a constructed pond on your premises can provide lifelong enrichment to your Mallard ducks and prove to be a wise investment.

Selecting an existing pond for the ducks

The decision to construct a pond may be rewarding, but is still expensive and complicated to undertake. It is perhaps for this reason that most free-range breeders prefer to adapt an already-existing pond in an available space for their Mallard ducks. In theory, a naturally existing pond should be perfect for the flock - it provides them with enough water to drink, bathe and swim. However, not all ponds may adhere to the conditions required by the ducks, especially if they have been previously misused.

If the pond has been a favourite fishing or picnic spot, you may find stray debris that has either sunk to the bottom or still floats around the surface. Any harmful stray objects can injure or damage your curious Mallards. Items such as empty cans or discarded construction material can also contain toxic substances that are hazardous to your ducks. Old forgotten fishing lines can also be death traps that ensnare your ducks and cause them to drown.

Once you have cleared away your pond, pay attention to how accessible it is to your ducks. Mallard ducks, due to their body size, require low, gently sloping land for easy navigation. A gentle bank built into a corner will give your ducks an entry and exit point, as well as a safe spot near the pond to rest.

One of the main attractions of a natural pond to duck breeders is the abundance of forage material it provides. From weeds and grasses, to tiny insects and fish, a natural pond is an ideal food foraging resource for your Mallard ducks. You can however, increase the forage potential of your pond by planting additional flora that doesn't need much tending to. Tall grassy spaces on the banks will also give the ducks extra hiding spaces.

Some duck owners like to bring pond companions such as frogs or turtles for their duck pets. This is not a bad decision, but is one that significantly impacts the yield of your pond. Introducing extra fauna to the surroundings means your ducks will now share their food, water and oxygen sources with other species. If you want to maintain adequate feeding conditions for all your animals, you may then have to plant more floras.

Several other factors come into play when determining how ideal your pond is for your Mallard ducks. The amount of sunlight your pond receives affects the growth of algae on the water surface. Sunlight also plays an important part in preventing the water from freezing over during the cold months.

Your geographical location and its climatic conditions also impact how hospitable your pond is. Deep ponds can still sustain plant and animal life if they freeze in winter, but shallow ones will be harmful to your ducks. If you live in a warm area, however, the depth of your pond will not matter as much to your adult Mallards.

Chapter Seven: Feeding your Pet Duck

Mallard ducks are not fussy eaters; in fact, you will be surprised at how hearty their appetites are and how diverse their palates can be. However, you should not share their non-fussy attitude towards their feed. The health of your flock largely depends on their feeding habits, and as their caretaker, it is your responsibility to ensure your Mallard ducks receive the best available diet.

What to feed your Mallard ducks

You may have fed slices of bread to the ducks at a public park; understand that your Mallard ducks cannot live on scraps alone. Just as you would put effort into feeding your dog or cat specific types of food, the food that Mallard ducks receive requires equal thought.

To make matters convenient for you and your ducks, you can choose to provide feed that is manufactured to suit their health requirements. While this form of diet is sufficient for your ducks' well-being, you can also encourage them to find their own food by foraging in their surrounding areas.

a. Natural Forage

Essentially, Mallard ducks can survive perfectly well on the food that you provide. To encourage well-rounded development in your Mallard ducks, however, it is wise to guide them towards finding their own food sources. This practice helps your ducks stay alert, active and stress-free. Furthermore, guiding your ducks to feed on natural forage such as flies, mosquitoes, spiders and worms is an economical way to control the spread of pests in your area. Mallard ducks also feed on weeds and some forms of algae, helping maintain the flora in the area.

It has been observed that foraging habits vary in the ducks based on the weather conditions and time of day. Mallard ducks prefer to forage for food when the earth is warm enough to draw out prey. Depending on where you live, the ducks may forage for food either in the early hours or in the afternoon. Observe their preferences before you set out a time for foraging.

The only downside to encouraging natural forage is that your ducks may not be able to differentiate between the food they can and cannot consume. For these purpose, you may have to restrict their access to vegetation that you require, such as flowers, fruits and vegetables. So long as you can exercise some control over the foraging ground, this practice to supplement the ducks' diet is a healthy one.

b. Commercially Prepared Foods

As beneficial as natural foraging may be for your the well-being of your Mallard duck, in a domestic setting, it works best only as a supplement to your duck's diet. Your own settings may not have adequate foraging sources, and the ducks' curious natures may prompt them to wander too far from your premises.

You will still need to be the primary provider of food for your flock. By supplying your ducks with the right amount of food at scheduled times, you can prevent them from relying too heavily on natural forage. Your most reliable feeding options for this purpose are commercially manufactured foods prepared especially for the ducks.

Besides containing carefully calculated quantities of your ducks' daily nutritional requirement, commercially manufactured feed also helps rear your ducks to your suiting, if you are breeding them for husbandry purposes. Mallard ducks require different forms of nutrition depending on their age, gender and role in animal husbandry.

If you have to feed hatchlings and younger members, you have to include significant amounts of tissue building protein. Protein is especially important if you are raising Mallard ducks for their eggs. Ideally, protein forms about 28 per cent of a growing Mallard duck's diet, which can be provided through special "starter-feed" packs.

As the ducks age and progress past five weeks, they can progress to foods that substitute excess protein for other essential nutrients. These packs, usually called "breeder packs" include such essential minerals as calcium, needed by the female ducks for lay eggs. No matter what the dietary needs of your Mallard ducks are, commercially manufactured feed in today's times can ensure that they are met.

A common mistake that amateur duck owners make is to assume that the feed manufactures for a certain bird is suitable to all birds in general. When selecting feed for your Mallard ducks, ensure that is has been prepared for the ducks alone, and not for other birds such as chickens.

Chicken feed in particular, is usually boosted with medicines meant to fortify them, and these medicines will adversely affect Mallard ducks. If you are unable to find feed specifically designed for your ducks, try to prepare your own food blend. We will discuss what foods are right for your ducks in the following pages to give you an idea of how to prepare feed for your ducks at home.

If all else fails, you can always contact your duck seller, waterfowl expert or breeder for advice. These are people who are invested in the health and welfare of Mallard ducks, and can correctly guide you towards finding the right feed in your area or preparing your own.

c. The role of Grit in duck feed

Mallard ducks, like some other birds, digest their food with the help of an organ called the ventriculus, or the gizzard. This organ, however, requires further assistance to help break down bigger particles of food. Sand, tiny particles of dirt and other such grainy objects collected by the ducks while foraging make for perfect teeth-like substitutes for Mallard ducks.

Mallard ducks who forage in the wild can collect their own sand or grainy dirt - commonly known as grit. When you are the sole provider of food for your ducks, however, they have no means of finding sufficient grit for their gizzards.

You may not notice it immediately, but the amount of grit a duck consumes greatly affects the performance of their gizzards. The more grainy substances the ducks have to break down harder food, the more efficient their gizzards become. The organs also tend to increase in size with additional exercise, helping to build a healthy and strong digestive system in your Mallard duck.

To ensure that your ducks can consume a variety of foods with relative ease, provide them with a steady supply of grit within easy access. If your ducks are allowed to roam outdoors, you do not have to worry about providing any grit for them. If they have been housed indoors, it becomes your responsibility to tend to their needs.

You do not have to fret about mixing your own grit, or determining what materials are safe for your duck to consume. Nearly all vendors that supply duck feed also store especially manufactured bags of grit for your Mallard ducks. You can simply place a separate bowl of grit near the feeding containers and let your ducks collect the materials as they require.

Ensure that you do not mix the grit directly with their food; Mallard ducks consume grit at different times than food and mixing them together might cause your duck to swallow the dirt instead of storing it in its gizzard.

d. The need for Oyster Shells in duck feed

Calcium is a vital mineral for any growing animal; it helps to build and fortify bone structure. Mallard ducks, too require significant amounts of calcium during their developing years. Female Mallards, in particular, demand a special supply of calcium for better egg-laying once they reach maturation.

The interesting feature about calcium, however, is that its intake needs to be carefully monitored. A deficiency of calcium can produce brittle eggs and weaker bone structure in your Mallard females. Eggs that are laid may not hatch if not provided with enough calcium. An excess amount of calcium is just as harmful, which many instances of kidney failure in ducks traced back to excessive intake of this mineral.

Adult drakes and females who are not laying eggs will need far less calcium that their egg-laying community members. You will ,therefore, have to be alert towards the amount of calcium each member of your flock receives.
Those members that do not need large amounts of calcium will find the mineral in commercially manufactured feed, or even in their daily plants and natural forage. You will need to pay close attention to the calcium intake of your Mallard egg-laying females.

A common source of calcium preferred by many duck breeders is oyster shell. When crushed into tiny pieces, these shells can not only add calcium to the ducks' diet, but also provide them with a gritty substance for their gizzards. Ensure that the shell bowls are placed separately from the feeding and water bowls, so your ducks can consume them as per their needs.

If you cannot find oyster shell, you can also opt for cuttlebone, another rich and common source of calcium. Cuttlebone will require some preparation in the form of careful crushing, but will make for a perfect calcium supplement.

Since calcium is an essential yet tricky mineral to navigate around, any doubts that you may have regarding its intake should be addressed with your waterfowl expert. They will be able to correctly guide you and prevent any calcium-related mishaps from occurring within your flock.

Checklist of food items acceptable for your Mallard Ducks

Fruits	Vegetables	Nuts, seeds, legumes	Grasses, shrubs, plants	Other live feed
Black berries	Collard greens	Wheat	Dandelion	Crickets
Blueb erries	Romaine lettuce	Barley	Clover	Mealworm s
Logan berries	Radicchio	Cracke d corn	Bermuda grass	Superwor ms
Cranb erries	Carrots	Popcor n	Winter rye grass	Waxworm s
BOyse nberri es	Broccoli	Oats	Fescue grass	Silkworms
Pears	Cabbage	Rice	Zoysia grass	Earthwor ms
Squas h	Cauliflower	Millet	Blue grass	Nightcraw lers
Pump kin	Asparagus	Peas	Centipede grass	Red wigglers
Apple	Kale	Green beans, cooked	Rye grass	Moths

Papaya	Beets	Lima beans, cooked	Kikuyu grass	Leeches
Grapes	Sprouts	Snow peas, cooked	Blue grama grass	Cockroaches
Pineapple		Pinto beans, cooked	Dallis grass	Grasshoppers
Watermelon		Sunflower seeds	Wintergrass	Guppies
Eggplant		Safflower seeds	Wheatgrass	Minnows
Peaches		Sesame seeds	Crab grass	Goldfish
Cucumber		Pumpkin seeds	Tall oat grass	
Figs		Assorted bird seeds	Orchard leaves	
Cantaloupe			Grape leaves	
Persimmon				

Frequency

Mallard ducks have healthy appetites and need to be fed on a daily basis. A balanced diet for your ducks should comprise a healthy mix of commercially-manufactured feed, natural forage and any other scraps that you provide from your household. Apart from the content of the feed, however, the frequency of food supply is crucial to the well-being of your ducks.

Your ducks will quickly let you know when their preferred times for natural foraging are. During these warm periods of the day, your ducks will satisfy their hunger by feeding on insects, grasses, grit and other naturally available material. You can then take cues from their patterns to determine how you will supply the commercial part of their feed.

There are a number of ways to ensure that your ducks are fed on a daily basis. If you have the time and patience, you can supply them with fresh food during each feeding session, minimizing their need for natural foraging. Then there are breeders and owners who encourage food scouting in their ducks by placing their feed out in the late afternoon post-foraging hours.

You can also adopt the strategy of the more lenient breeders, and leave food containers out by the ducks' housing at all times. With this strategy, you let the Mallard ducks control how the quantity of food they intake. This convenient method usually works for all involved parties, but requires some maintenance on your part.

Housing pens that have round-the-clock feeding zones generally tend to becomes messier at a faster rate. You will have to maintain hygienic standards by cleaning out the food and water trays regularly, as well as clear away inevitable droppings from nearby areas. You also have to ensure that your ducks' feed is supplemented with plenty of clean water.

The Importance of Freshness

Save for a few exceptions, you can exercise a lot of flexibility when it comes to your ducks' feed. One of the only factors you cannot compromise on is the freshness of your feed. Old or stale feed is susceptible to fungal growth that may make your ducks very ill. Furthermore, mould can grow on just about any type of food - from your fresh produce to your commercially-bought food packets.

The best way to ensure fresh feed for your ducks is to find a reliable vendor and stick with them. Before every purchase, take a minute to check if the bags are sealed and the food has been recently produced. If you find that the price of the feed has been discounted drastically, pay close attention to the expiry date and contents of the feed. Some vendors may offer older stocks at lower prices to clear their shelves faster.

You may also be attracted to larger quantities of feed that provide greater "value for money". Before you purchase this feed, you should understand that the feed catches mould incredibly early once it has been opened. Larger bags of food are a smart choice if you have a big flock, but may not be best for a small group.

The right storage conditions also help to keep your feet fresh for longer. The bag is good enough to store the feed in, but if you're using the feed for a long time, transfer them into airtight containers, preferably marked with the expiry dates.

Every so often, take an inventory of the feed you have stored aside. If expired food is harmful to your health, it is equally bad for your Mallard ducks. Do not feed them any food that has spoiled, collected mold or its past its shelf-life.

If a major portion of your feed comprises of fresh produce, you can store these items in sealable bags and freeze them for weeks, even months. It may take some effort to constantly maintain fresh food options, but you will be rewarded with healthy, happy and high-yielding Mallard ducks.

What not to feed your Mallard ducks

Once you settle into a feeding pattern with your Mallard ducks, you may find that their palates are surprisingly easy to please. In such instances, some people begin shirking their strict dietary responsibility, feeding Mallard ducks any food available in their surroundings.

If you want to avoid health hazards among your flock, however, you should understand that you have a lifelong dietary commitment to uphold. Not only do you ensure that your provide food and water on a regular basis, you also ensure that your Mallard ducks stay away from the following foods:

1. Medicated duck feeds may seem like a smart dietary addition to your duck's feed, but is unnecessary unless prescribed by your waterfowl expert. These specifically engineered feeds contain medicines that may be too strong for healthy Mallard ducks.

2. Bread is not only a source of minimal nutrition to us, but also to Mallard ducks. Composed mainly of empty calories and sugar, ducks have a weakness for bread, and will ignore any nutritious food in its presence. Copious amounts of bread will fatten up your ducks without providing them with any useful nutrition. In their excitement, your ducks may also try to swallow too much dry bread, which could lead to choking.

3. Foods that are rich in oxalic acids such as spinach, almonds, and chocolate may be good for you, but are bad for Mallard ducks, particularly females. These foods can absorb the calcium content from your feed, weaken the quality of the ducks' eggshells.

4. Certain fruits may be too acidic for your Mallard ducks, and cause digestive issues. Citric fruits such as oranges, lemons, and grapefruit are best not fed to your ducks.

5. Other fresh produce that may be healthy for you but is incredibly toxic for Mallard ducks includes avocados, onions, shallots and chives. These foods can cause a variety of ailments, ranging from digestive problems and cardiac ailments.

6. Chocolate is also known to be highly toxic for Mallard ducks and can lead to poisoning, convulsions, nervous disorders, and death.

7. Processed foods that are high in salts, sugar and unhealthy fats are just as bad for your Mallard ducks as they are for you. While they may not be toxic for the ducks, even tiny portions of processed foods may be too fatty for them.

8. Fatty foods in general are best kept away from your Mallard ducks. Along with avocados and fatty processed foods, nuts should also be avoided. Along with filling your ducks with fatty content they don't require, nuts also may become trapped in the ducks' bills and choke them.

Mallard ducks and toxic vegetation

While we can have considerable information on the health effects that basic fruits and vegetables have on Mallard ducks' health, we still haven't completely understood which plants bring about toxic reactions in the birds.

Based on their ability to adapt to almost any type of environment, it is generally believed that Mallard ducks are immune to the toxicity in most, if not all plants. Breeders, naturalists, behaviourists and other experts are still trying to ascertain whether this immunity to toxic plants is a physical ability or an instinctual one.

Therefore, while you're Mallard ducks may not be able to reveal toxic vegetation in your area; you should take the time to inspect the plant life that your ducks will be housed in. Even if the ducks themselves avoid being poisoned, you could easily come into contact with these plants while handling your ducks.

You can also speak to the local flora and waterfowl experts to discover what local plants may be harmful to your duck, if any. Familiarize yourself with common plant life in your region to help avoid any mishaps among your flock.

Common Name	Scientific Name
Amaryllis	*Amaryllis belladonna*
Anemone	*Anemone* sp.
Anthurium	*Anthurium*sp.
Asparagus Fern	*Asparagus sprengeri*
Arrowhead Vine	*Syngoniumpodophyllum*
Atamasco Lily	*Zephyranthes*sp.
Azalea	*Rhododendron sp.*
Autumn Crocus	*Colchicum autumnale*
Avocado	*Perseaamericana*
Baneberry	*Actaea*sp.
Begonia	*Begonia* sp.
Bird of Paradise	*Poinciana gilliesii*
Black Cherry	*Prunusserotina*
Black Locust	*Robiniapseudoacacia*
Black Nightshade	*Solanumnigrum*
Black Snakeroot	*Zigadenus*sp.
Bleeding Heart	*Dicentraspectabilis*
Bloodroot	*Sanguinariacanadensis*
Boxwood	*Buxus*sp
Boston Ivy	*Parthenocissustricuspidata*
Buttercup	*Ranunculus* sp.
Butterfly Weed	*Asclepias*sp.
Caladium	*Caladium* sp.
Calla Lily	*Zantedeschia* sp.
Candytuft	*Iberis*sp.
Cardinal Flower	*Lobelia cardinalis*

Carolina Jasmine	*Gelsemiumsempervirens*
Castor Beans	*Ricinuscommunis*
Cherry Laurel	*Prunuscaroliniana*
Chinaberry	*Meliaazedarach*
Christmas Rose	*Helleborusniger*
Clematis	*Clematis* sp.
Coriander	*Coriandrumsativum*
Corn Cockle	*Agrostemmagithago*
Cowslip	*Calthapalustris*
Daffodil	*Narcissus* sp.
Delphinium	*Delphinium* sp.
Elderberry	*Sambucus*sp.
English Ivy	*Hedera helix*
Four O'clock	*Mirabilis jalapa*
Foxglove	*Digitalis purpurea*
Giant Elephant Ear	*Alocasia*sp.
Gloriosa Lily	*Gloriosasuperba*
Golden Chain Tree	*Laburnum anagyroides*
Goldenseal	*Hydrastiscanadensis*
Henbane	*Hyoscyamusniger*
Holly	*Ilex* sp.
Horse Chestnut	*Aesculus*sp.
Hyacinth	*Hyacinthusorientalis*
Hydrangeas	*Hydrangea* sp.
Ivy (Common / English)	*Hedera helix*
Irises	*Iris* sp.
Jack-In-The-Pulpit	*Arisaematriphyllum*
Jerusalem Cherry	*Solanumpseudocapsicum*
Junipers / Red Cedars	*Juniperus* sp.
Lily of the Nile	*Agapanthus africanus*
Lily of the Valley	*Convallaria* sp.
Lobelia	*Lobelia* sp.
Lucky Nut	*Thevetiaperuviana*
Lupine	*Lupinus*sp.
Marijuana	*Cannabis* sp.

Meadow Buttercup	*Ranunculus acris*
Milkweed	*Asclepias*sp.
Mistletoe	*Viscum*sp.
Mock Orange	*Philadelphus*sp.
Mountain Laurel	*Kalmia latifolia*
Mourning Glory	Family*Convolvulaceae*
Nandina	*Nandinaadomestica*
Nightshades	*Solanum* sp.
Parsley	*Petroselinumcrispum*
Periwinkle	*Vinca minor* and *V. major*
Philodendron	*Philodendron* sp.
Pittosporum	*Pittosporum*sp.
Poinsettia	*Euphorbia pulcherrima*
Potato Plants	*Solanumtuberosum*
Pothos	*Pothos* sp.
Primrose	*Primula*sp.
Privet	*Ligustrum*sp.
Rapeseed	*Brassica napus*
Rhubarb (leaves)	*Rheum rhabarbarum*
Rosary Bean	*Abrusprecatarius*
Schefflera	*Schefflera*sp.
Shasta Daisy	*Chrysanthemum maximum*
Sorghum	*Sorghum* sp.
Spider Mum	*Chrysanthemum morifolium*
Split Leaf Philodendron	*Monsteradeliciosa*
Spring Adonis	*Adonis vernalis*
St. John's Wort	*Hypericumperforatum*
Strawberry Bush	*Euonymous* sp.
Tobacco	*Nicotiana*sp.
Trumpet Flower	*Solandra*sp.
Umbrella Tree	*Scheffleraactinophylla*
Water Hemlock	*Cicutamaculata*
Weeping Yew	*Taxus*sp.
Wisteria	*Wisteria* sp.

source: www.allthedirtongardening.com

Chapter Eight: Interacting with Your Pet Duck

At the outset, it is essential to understand that interacting with a Mallard duck is very different from interacting with other pet animals. Mallard ducks, in fact, tend to behave differently than other domestic duck species as well! This does not mean that Mallard ducks cannot be domesticated or interacted with; simply that handling your Mallard duck requires special care and attention.

By nature, Mallard ducks tend to be quite defensive and extremely proud of their physical size. This is perhaps best exhibited by their aversion for being picked up. Accustomed to being among the larger birds among their kind, Mallard ducks will become defensive if you try to pick them too often. They use their toenails and beaks to cause sharp and painful injuries to anyone who invades their personal space.

If this pecking and vigorous wing-flapping won't deter you, perhaps a sharp gust of pungent-smelling discharge from their posterior tract will. As part of their defensive arsenal, Mallard ducks have the ability to emit out the half-solid, half-liquid contents from their cloaca to release an odour that can effectively disperse a small crowd in the vicinity. When you raise and breed Mallard ducks as your own, you will soon adapt to the foul nature of this smell, sometimes found even on the eggs.

It becomes obvious, then, that Mallard ducks are not to be picked and cuddled as if they were kittens, puppies or hamsters. If you have children in your household or neighbourhood, it is essential that you explain the proud natures of these ducks to them. Ducklings are relatively safer to pick up and interact with, although they require their own set of interaction guidelines.

Do not let the suspicious and proud natures of the Mallard ducks deter you, however. While it may be tricky, you certainly can use simple techniques to help physically interact with your duck. With time, patience and respect for your Mallard ducks, you can raise them to view you as non-threatening, and even make them loyal towards you. Through this chapter, we will explore the many way through which you can initiate enough contact with your Mallard ducks to form a lifelong loving bond with them.

Interacting with Ducklings

During the few months of their lives, Mallard ducklings require to be shifted from one spot to another, for various purposes. Handling these ducklings is relatively easier than holding and lifting adult ducks, mostly due to their size and the ineffectiveness of their pecking.

Furthermore, the cloaca of the ducklings has still not developed enough for their contents to be odorous, so you only have to deal with a small amount of poop! Since the ducklings are tiny, you can also lift them in a way that ensures their cloaca is facing away from you.

When you pick up a Mallard duckling, be as delicate as possible. It is best to pick up the ducklings by scooping them up from their sides, either with one palm or both. Do not enclose them tightly within your palm; instead form safe cocoons with your inner palm that gives the duckling warmth and discourages it from flapping its wings. Based on the size of your duckling, you can either gently fold their feet beneath them in your palms, or even let them dangle between cracks in your fingers.

The ducklings will likely peck at your fingers during the first few interactions, but their beaks are harmless to adults and many children as well. In addition, the more your duckling is handles by you, the more he will adapt to your presence, and with time, the pecking will gradually recede to a stop.

Lifting, Holding, Transporting and Catching Your Duck

It doesn't matter if you've been holding your Mallard duck since the day it was born; as an adult, a Mallard duck will discourage you from holding it as much as it can. You may wisely want to give your ducks their freedom and not hold them too often, but certain circumstances will require you to lift, hold and even examine them for injuries and ailments.

In such situations, it is smart to replicate the calm demeanour of your Mallard duck. Any sudden movements, noise or a large group of people will agitate your duck. The best way to hold your duck is to approach it stealthily during the darker hours of the day. Mallard ducks experience a strange sense of disorientation when they have no light, and can be picked up without being startled. If you need to hold your duck during the daytime, place them in a dark room for about an hour, and then approach them with caution.

You may be as stealthy as a cat, and quiet as a whisper, and may still find it next to impossible to catch your duck - don't be disheartened. Mallard ducks take great pride in their ability to evade capture due to their suspicious natures, which makes them very agile. In these cases, create tunnels to enclose the ducks in their nesting boxes using cardboard boxes. Let the tunnels become narrower as the duck moves through them, till it reaches a point through which it cannot pass. Here, you can gently intervene and lift your duck.

Lifting your Mallard duck

Once you do manage to approach your Mallard duck, lifting them the right way is of utmost importance. Remember, an adult Mallard is significantly larger and heavier than a young one, so its defence mechanisms are likely to hurt you more. Another point to remember is that Mallard ducks cannot be lifted the same way as other domestic birds, such as chickens. Do not attempt to lift them by their feet; you will cause them severe injury, possibly even a fracture.

The smartest way to lift your Mallard duck is replicate the movements used to grab it as a duckling. Enclose the body from the sides with your hands in a calm and slow movement. When you lift the bird, its wings should rest neatly and firmly against its body to prevent the duck form flapping them about. As your Mallard duck is heavy, you will also need support its weight from under, by placing a hand beneath its feet. This clasp also prevents the duck from clawing at you with its toenails.

Whether you leave the duck's toes dangling from your fingers or fold it under their bodies depends on your preference. Either method of holding the duck is comfortable for it, provided you don't apply too much pressure. Hold the duck close to your body to help secure one wing, while enclosing the other wing with the hand that clasps the feet. This method will free up one hand for tasks in your surroundings.

Once you have finished examining your duck, place it back down as calmly and gently as you can. Sudden and quick movements may cause the duck to become agitated and even result in injuries as they land.

Ushering around your Mallard duck

As much as you may enjoy picking up and cuddling a younger Mallard duck, understand that the affectionate stops almost as soon as the Mallard duck comes of age. Once your duck is mature, they will most likely avoid all your attempts at lifting or handling them. During this time, it is best to give Mallard ducks their freedom of space and movement.

It is still, however, important that you channel your ducks' movements to your needs, as you may need them to move to certain areas for feeding, bathing or medical aid. Instead of trying to physically place them in your desired spots, you will find more success if subtly guide the ducks to the required spot.

Active birds though they may be, Mallard ducks are also extremely wilful, and do not like to be told where to go. However, you can easily manipulate their will by taking advantage of their strict routine-friendly natures. Mallard ducks prefer specified areas and timings for feeding, drinking, bathing and nesting.

If you need them to remain active during the day, simply make a habit of closing the entrance to their nesting space as soon as they leave. Ensure that your determined spots for eating, drinking, bathing and nesting are consistent. With routine closure, the ducks will soon learn to return to their homes only when night falls.

If you follow a strict orderly schedule with your Mallard ducks, you will find it alarmingly easy to herd them towards their daily tasks. With specific times and areas for each activity, Mallard ducks will go about their daily lives without needing assistance on your behalf. Each evening, they will return to the nesting zone, pretty much of their own volition.

While they will never top any intelligence charts in the animal kingdom, Mallard ducks are surprisingly smart when routines and fixed routes are involved. They have the ability to adapt to any schedule that is comfortable for you, so long as it is consistent and instilled in them from a young age. Mallard ducks also grasp behaviour by imitating what they observe. Therefore, it is easiest to train newer ducks by placing them with ducks who have already been trained.

Amusingly enough, Mallard ducks respond well to bribes, especially if these are supplied at the same time each day. To convince a duck to leave the nesting zone, therefore, all you need to do is place some food at the entrance, and then have the duck follow the food to your desired area. With a few days of practice and conditioning, the duck will learn to arrive at your desired spot at the required time.

Not all Mallard ducks can be bribed with tasty morsels of food, however. You will have a member or two who does not succumb to bribes or prefers to scamper away when approached. Here is a simple step-by-step approach to help you handle these mischievous ducks:

1. Begin your approach from a distance of about 17-18 meters. Enclose the duck within your required space by circling the immediate area around them. You should aim to be an obstacle between the duck and its escape.

2. Your territory should enclose the duck within it, but also encourage the duck to go in your intended direction. To do this, place yourself in the exact opposite direction to the one you intend your duck to travel to.

3. Now, make your way towards the Mallard duck in small, slow and deliberate movements. In response, the Mallard duck will automatically move in the opposite direction, in this case the direction of your choice. If you already have other ducks moving in that direction, your duck will take a cue from them and join the group.

4. In case you're Mallard duck starts of in the right direction but wanders away to the wrong spot, guide his movements by using the opposite placement manoeuver. As a guiding tool, you can also bring along a stick, to tap near the duck and encourage it to move in the opposite direction.

5. For instance, if you want the duck to head towards the right, place the stick close to the left side of the duck, and

tap the ground. Do not touch the duck with the stick as you may startle it. The gentle sounds will drive the duck to move in the right direction.

If chasing after your ducks and herding them around is too time-consuming for you, you can easily domesticate and train an animal, such as a dog for this purpose. Many duck owners, in fact, prefer keeping a guard dog to watch over their flocks, two if necessary. Guard dogs not only help usher your ducks around, but also help to keep your ducks safe from predators, while maintaining a peaceful atmosphere within the flock.

Transporting Your Pet

As comfortable as their home environments may be, you will face many instances during which you will have to take your Mallard ducks out of their surroundings. These may include trips to the local waterfowl expert, or even a short journey to the local county fair to win a prize for most beautiful duck! Whatever be the circumstance, transporting your Mallard duck is an issue of importance, although the solutions for this are fairly simple.

a. Plastic Tubs

Plastic tubs are the cheapest, and also the simplest means through which you can comfortably cart your Mallard ducks around. All your transportation tub requires is a roof that prevents the ducks from flying during transportation. You then drill a few well-placed holes into the roof and the side walls, in order to facilitate air flow in the tub. Make the bottom comfortable for the duck by cushioning the surface with piles of straw, grass or even paper. These materials will also absorb and hold any wet or waste material produced by your Mallard duck.

The only factor to keep in mind is that your ducks should be as stress-free as possible. Since their stress is often caused by unhygienic conditions, ensure that there is plenty of fresh air flowing through the tub to keep your duck from falling sick. To further guarantee a stress-free ride, try and provide opaque transportation tubs for your Mallard ducks. These will shield your ducks away from the outside world, while the dark tones will help them relax. If you must use translucent or transparent tubs, try and cover them with a light cloth to provide some obstacle.

b. Wire Cages

As comfortable as plastic tubs may be, it is the wire cages that are a preferred mode of transportation for Mallard duck owners. It is easy to see why wire cages are highly favored - with large airy spaces, there is little need to provide your own source of ventilation for the ducks. Furthermore, wire cages are easier to carry around and come readily manufactured to suit a variety of needs and preferences. While a perfect transportation option in warmer climates, wire cages can quickly become an inconvenience.

The openness of the cages makes it significantly colder and uncomfortable for the ducks within the cage. Furthermore, open wire cages are also a messier affair than their plastic counterparts. With an open free space, it is easy for such particles as stray food, droppings and shedding to simply spill out of the cage. These cages may also need to be covered up to prevent the ducks from becoming stressed due to a change in the outside environment.

c. Tips to ensure safe Mallard duck transportation

1. Secure your transportation container to your vehicle to prevent it from sliding around and causing either stress or a mess. You can do this by buckling the seat belt around the container, or even use heavy-duty straps or bungee cords. This safety measure will ensure that your ducks are not thrown around the vehicle in case of turbulence.

2. Do not leave your Mallard ducks inside a vehicle with the windows sealed shut. Just as with humans, the rising heat within a sealed glass space can be uncomfortable and even harmful to your Mallard ducks. Leaving them unattended in a hot confined space may even lead to their death, as has been seen many times before.

3. Try to avoid transporting your ducks with a large group of people, as the noise and crowd may be unsettling for the ducks. Loud music and other disturbing behaviour is also known to be stressful to the ducks.

4. Finally, ensure that you drive as steadily and responsibly as possible. You do not want to startle and agitate your ducks with rash driving - the results will be loud and unpleasant both for you and the ducks!

Interacting with aggressive Mallard drakes

The breeding season is a highly stressful one for the Mallard drake. He spends much of these months warding off competition from other drakes to impregnate the Mallard ducks. This tends to make the drakes quite hostile to nearly everyone they interact with, including their keepers, on occasion.

Understand that your Mallard drake does not suddenly "hate" you; he is simply trying to assert his dominance in a social situation. If there are no other drakes in your flock, the Mallard drake will probably view you as competition, even if you are a woman. Reacting to his hormonal impulses before anything else, a Mallard drake may charge at or even chase you when he spots you. If you are close, he may aggressively attack you with his wings to drive you away. If you are patient, you can easily wait till the breeding season ends for your drake to behave himself again.

Some people, however, may find this behaviour alarming, even frightening. In other cases, you may need to approach your drake during the breeding season for a variety of reasons. If you cannot wait the breeding season out, you will need to engage in a little "war-of-dominance" with your drake.

There are two basic strategies for dealing with this problem. The first is to simply provide the duck with some extra space until his hormones calm down. However, this is not always possible. In such cases, it may be more effective to restrain the bird.

Your role in this war of dominance is not to hurt the drake; simply to make him believe that you are the "alpha-male" in this surrounding. As is the case with dominant males, you will assert your authority by holding your ground when the drake charges at you. Do not step back or waver in your stance; the drake views this act as submission. If you must, hold the drake down by his sides when he is close to you and gently pin him to the floor till he submits. You should be extremely careful that you don't harm the drake in this procedure, as it may traumatize him. Treat this exercise as a playful event with your drake in which you show him who is boss. As soon as the drake realizes you can overpower him, he will stop charging at you and carry on his bullying acts elsewhere.

Mallard ducks and the Imprinting phenomenon

Of all the interactions that you have with your Mallard duck, it is the process of imprinting that will have the most impact on your bond. The phenomenon of imprinting in Mallard ducks is so unique and complicated that study is still underway to completely grasp this peculiar behaviour. However, constant observation and study has given us the basic understanding that Mallard ducks form lifelong imprints in two significant areas:

a.   Filial Imprinting

Filial imprinting, in simple terms, the permanent parental bond that Mallard ducks form as hatchlings. While most species are able to tell their own kind apart from others almost from the moment of birth, this is not so with Mallard ducks. Furthermore, many other species can be later trained to identify with their own kind (as in the case of dogs, cats, etc.), but not so with Mallard ducks.

It is due to this quirk that Mallard hatchlings will identify the first living being they see as their mother. If you have opted for natural incubation, or are unaware of a nesting egg, the duckling may see its real mother and make the right connection. If you are the first person the hatchling sees, however, it becomes your permanent responsibility to "parent" the duckling.

The process of imprinting wires the duck's brains so uniquely, that the creature becomes almost besotted with its parental figure. From following it around, to adopting its mannerisms, a filial imprint makes the duckling completely devoted to their parent. If your duckling has imprinted on you, expect it to be a shadow that requires feeding and attention.

Many people argue that filial imprinting in ducks is not that different to the loyal connection that dogs, cats or other domestic animals feel towards humans; this is not entirely true. While filial imprinting does make the duck loyal to their owner, it also takes away the duck's ability to distinguish itself from its parent. No matter how attached your dog or cat is to you, it will still know who its mother is, and will recognize its kind as its own.

If you're Mallard duck adopts you as its parent, however, it will also begin to see itself as a human. Similarly, if your duckling forms a filial imprint on your dog or cat, expect it to take on that animal's mannerisms! Amusing as it may be, filial imprinting still makes it tricky when you need your duck to be social. You will need to help your duck interact with others in its flock to help it forms brotherly connections with other ducks. While some of these communal feelings may later become sexual, your Mallard duck will never forget its parent and will always be the most loyal to them.

b.   Sexual Imprinting

Filial imprinting, apart from the reasons stated above is also crucial as it plays a fundamental role in the sexual imprint your Mallard duck will form. In general, sexual imprinting is important because it helps any living animal distinguished attractive features among its kind for reproduction. Because our Mallard duck friends imprint in interesting ways, sexual imprinting is an equally unique experience for them.

With Mallard ducks, it is the parental figure's species that they adopt as their own. If your duckling has imprinted on a duck for a parent, they will grow up to find other ducks sexually attractive. If you have become the adopted parent of the duck, however, it is your kind that the duck looks to sexually imprint on. In such cases, it become your responsibility to guide the ducks towards the right sexual imprint.

We already know that regardless of the filial imprint of the duckling, you can help it interact and form bonds with other ducks as well. If your duckling has been surrounded by other ducks since birth, it will then grow to find these familiar features sexually attractive. If raised in isolation, however, Mallard ducks will likely imprint on their parental figure, even if it is human in form.

It is for reasons such as filial and sexual imprinting that Mallard ducks require more time, effort and commitment from you as an owner. If you have plans to hatch and raise the ducklings yourself, you take on the added role of parenting and nurturing the young ones into adulthood. This is why, it is first essential that you fully comprehend the three factors surrounding a duck's upbringing:

Dedicated time for the duckling

The responsibilities of a parental figure d not simply end at feeding and bathing the young. Just as your young one needs to be played with, cajoled and nurtured, so does a duckling who forms a filial imprint on you. Once you become the duckling's adopted parent, it becomes your duty to take care of its food, sleeping times and cleanliness. It is also you who comforts the stressed duckling, sleeps with it to provide cosiness and warmth, and helps it make new friends. Understand that you will have very little time away from the duck when its young - much like parenting a human baby.

Patience to nurture the duck

Mallard ducks may identify you as their parent, but will firmly stick on to their proud and defensive personalities. You cannot expect to toilet train your duck, and certainly cannot expect the duck to follow specific behavioural commands. No matter how possible you think it may be, it is you who will have to adapt to the nature of the duckling, instead of vice-versa. Cleaning their droppings constantly and ignoring their pecks will become bearable only with time and patience.

Resources to care for the duck

You may it adorable that your "duck-child" has taken on several of your mannerisms and believes itself to be human; this does not change the truth that it is still a duck. You cannot substitute its dietary and health-care needs simply because of filial imprinting. The Mallard duck will require its scheduled supply of food, water and exercise.
You will need to ensure that your space is as secure from predators as possible. You will need to provide a source of water and the highest quality of changing feed for the duck. Extra expenses are incurred in such matters as clipping wings, routine examinations and medical expenses.

And even when you have set up your surroundings perfectly for yourself and your pet, you still have to consider external factors such as your neighbour's acceptance of a noisy duck, and the ease with which the duck can adapt to unfamiliar surroundings.

When you do make the choice to bring home Mallard ducks, take the time to understand how imprinting will affect your future with duck. Every interaction you will have with your pet will be based on this unique characteristic trait, and it is your willingness to adapt to imprinting that will raise the quality of your Mallard duck's life.

Mallard ducks require a secure atmosphere in order to be comfortable and stress-free. In some cases, even the most secure and comfortable surroundings may not be enough to stop your ducks from trying to escape. Very often, the only solutions that successfully prevent your Mallard duck from flying away include pinioning and feather clipping.

c.   Pinioning

The process of pinioning requires a trained professional to extract particular section of the bird's wings. By doing so, you take away the bird's ability to fly, which is why this procedure is best undertaken when the ducks are young. Although an effective procedure, pinioning is a painful process and almost always a stressful experience for your duck. In many instances, pinioning is so traumatic for the duck that it dies not long after the event.

Not surprisingly, most duck owners find pinioning to be a cruel and unethical practice. Quite a few locations around the world, in fact, have rendered this practice illegal. Therefore, should you choose to pinion your duck's wings, ensure that it is allowed and is conducted by an expert in your area. You can also buy ducks whose wings have already been pinioned, if that is your preference.

d.   Feather Clipping

In case pinioning your duck is not your cup of tea, you can opt for the less painful practice of clipping your duck's feathers. Through this procedure, you cut off the essential features needed for flight, usually only on one side. This makes it difficult for the duck to fly, although not causing them any harm in the process.

Since it is a painless and simple procedure, most veterinary offices and pet shops will offer feather clipping services at reasonable rates, although you can perform it yourself. All you need is proper training under your waterfowl expert and the dedication to clip your duck's feather once annually. With a pair of sharp scissors and the knowledge of which feather to clip, you can ensure that that your duck remains within the premises without causing them trauma.

e.   Are these practices necessary?

Feather clipping and pinioning are only undertaken by those owners who want to prevent their ducks from escaping. As effective as they may be, these acts hinder your duck's ability to fly even in situations where they need to escape predators.

This is why many duck owners prefer to leave their ducks' wings untouched, even at the risk of them escaping. A full set of wings allow the Mallard duck to comfortably navigate its surroundings and evade capture from such animals as dogs, raccoon and foxes. Furthermore, a safe and healthy environment filled with other ducks will often be enough to keep the Mallard duck from leaving. The choice to "de-wing" your Mallard duck, or allow them to roam about freely, therefore, is a personal one that requires great thought and consideration for yourself as well as the Mallard duck.

Chapter Nine: Health Concerns for Mallard Ducks

Mallard ducks are among the stronger of aviary creatures and have immune systems that can withstand most form of illnesses and infection. Mallard ducks, however, are not infallible, and will become ill and infected if housed in extremely unhygienic conditions.

It may not always be possible to ensure that your ducks are free from ailments. The social nature of Mallard ducks brings them into contact with a host of objects and animals, capable of transmitting diseases. To help keep your ducks as healthy as possible, here are three essential guidelines recommended by the Centre for Diseases Prevention when caring for Mallard ducks:

1.   Minimize the contact and interaction your Mallard Ducks have with other species of ducks, birds or even animals. This will prevent new infections from entering as well as leaving the flock.

2.   Ensure that your ducks are in relaxed, stress-free settings. Any traumatic events in a ducks surrounding may adversely its health.

3.   Provide your ducks with timely vaccinations and health check-ups, to isolate any possible infection or ailment before it causes further damage.

Hygienic settings can go a long way in preventing the spread of disease and infection, but you may not always be able to protect your ducks from such unforeseen illnesses as fowl cholera. While milder infections can be treated in your ducks, severe ones such as fowl cholera can only be treated by eliminating the entire flock. Furthermore, sexual disorders such as egg binding are difficult to pinpoint due to the absence of any viral or bacterial infections or symptoms. Such ailments can only be treated with the help of your doctor.

Common Infections

While Mallard ducks are largely immune to most forms of poisoning, toxicity and infections that befall other poultry, they still are susceptible to certain infections brought on by bacteria and virus in their surroundings. While some illnesses have vaccinations and prepared medication, many infections require that your Mallard duck be put to sleep, sometimes with the rest of the flock. It is for these reasons that the maintenance of a hygiene space becomes crucial.

Name	Causes	Symptoms	Treatment
Cocci diosis	Protozoal infection	Digestive issues, secretion from the eyes, depression	Recently developed vaccine available at veterinary office
Avian influe nza	Viral infections that also communicate to other living beings	Damage to pancreas, nervous system impairment	Precautionary vaccinations available at veterinary office

Rieme rellaa natipe stifer	bacterial infection	intestinal trouble, secretions from eye, weight loss, collapsing on back with flailing legs	Preventive vaccination and medications available at veterinary office
Duck Viral Enteri tis	viral infection	gastrointestinal troubles, nasal discharge, lethargy, aversion to bright lights, anorexia, droopiness, death within hours	Preventive vaccination available at veterinary office
Haem oprote us	respiratory infection	varied to no visible symptoms	no effective isolated treatment
Fowl Chole ra	highly contagious bacteria Pasteurellam ultocida	Intestinal difficulties, depression, irregular breathing, anorexia	Depopulation of entire flock and cleansing of premises
Duck Parvo virus	transferable viral infection among younger Mallard ducks with	digestive troubles, nervousness ,agitation, shedding of feathers	No effective isolated treatment

	only 20 percent chance of survival		

Common Reproductive Disorders

Reproductive disorders can be especially excruciating for your Mallard ducks, especially the egg-laying females. Such disorders usually occur due to an imbalance in the hormonal functions of the duck. While certain cases such as exposed penis in male drakes can be treated quickly, ailments such as egg binding and oviduct prolapse, if left untreated, may result in death shortly after being stricken with the disorder.

Name of disease	Definition	Symptoms	Treatment
Egg binding	inability to pass egg due to injury to vagina, abnormal size of egg, or calcium deficiency, among other causes	difficulty in egg laying, nervous disposition, agitation, depression, abnormal gait or body posture, abrupt death	Immediate assistance from veterinarian

Oviduct Prolapse	silent in the oviduct due to improper passing of egg	protrusion of oviduct in the lower body	calcium and phosphorus supplements, warm conditions for duck, oral medication under veterinary prescription
Exposed Penis	inability to retract penis due to infection	drooping, protruding penis that is vulnerable to further infection	Sanitized and hygienic drinking water and living quarters
Meritis	bacterial infection in the oviduct that leads to inflammation	continuous vaginal discharge, lethargy, loss of appetite	antibodies given through injections or oral medication
Peritonitis	infection of peritoneum as a result of ovarian prolapse	abdominal swelling, diarrhea, abrupt death	antibodies given through oral medication

Mallard ducks and behavioural issues

Mallard ducks can be very calm and placid creatures, almost ideal pets to have around, provided the conditions are to the ducks' suiting. If you do observe any sudden behavioural changes in your duck, these can be attributed to two major factors - a change in the ducks' surroundings or within the ducts themselves.

Just as adolescents undergo a form of identity crisis just before maturation, so do many Mallard ducks face behavioural issues around their sixth month. This behaviour will usually signal your ducks' progress from a juvenile Mallard to an adult duck ready for mating. Behavioural changes to watch out for during this period include pecking, pinching, charging, and generally hostile behaviour.

Perturbing though this behaviour may be, understand that you can calm your ducks down and teach them to keep a check on their aggressive tendencies. Since Mallard ducks are creatures of habit, simple repetitive gestures during their "episodes" can help them understand their behaviour is not acceptable.

Mallard ducks are intelligent and perceptive enough that a sharp reprimand from you every time they behave badly will send a clear message. Try and use the same word and gesture to admonish your duck, such as "no" or "stop". Accompany this phrase with a subtly dominant gesture, such as holding your duck's bill gently shut and maybe even giving the bill a gentle nudge or pat.

These acts of dominance should never hurt your duck; simply let them know they're being unreasonable. Mallard ducks, especially drakes, tend to view all bigger living beings as competition or threats, so it is important to reassure them that you are neither. By kindly yet firmly asserting your authority, you can win over their trust and loyalty in no time.

The only other critical change in Mallard ducks' behavioural patterns occur when they undergo periods of severe stress. Ranging from reasons such as a change in the temperature to the arrival of new ducks, and even including serious health concerns, any abrupt difference in the routine of a Mallard duck may cause it to display such stressful symptoms as excessive wing-flapping in distress, shallow breathing with an open bill and even isolating themselves from other ducks. Any such significant differences in behaviour are causes for worry and should be addressed with your waterfowl expert immediately.

The Importance of Waterfowl Experts

Experienced and professional though they may be, veterinarians for animals such as cats, dogs, rabbits, hamsters etc. may not always be the best people to treat your Mallard ducks. These semi-aquatic creatures require special care from waterfowl experts who have specialized in and are more familiar with the health requirements of your ducks. The good news is, finding a waterfowl expert is an easy-enough process.

If you do not already have a waterfowl expert to contact, your Mallard duck sellers, retailers or breeders will all be happy to help you. Breeders and retailers usually have the best sources on call, since the health of their ducks is their top priority. If these options don't work out for you, however, some simple research of your own will yield plenty of results.

Many experts offering waterfowl health care services advertise on the Internet and can be located within a few minutes. Additionally, you can also rely on feedback and reviews from other duck breeders and owners to narrow down the best option for your Mallard ducks.

Once you find your waterfowl expert, it is best to take your ducks up to them for an initial examination. If you believe that taking your duck for a medical check-up is a simple matter of transporting the ducks in their cages, you're in for a big surprise! Mallard ducks, thanks to their sensitive natures, do not particularly enjoy a ride to the veterinarian's office. To help keep your ducks as calm as possible, try to find an expert who is willing to make house calls, especially if you own a flock of ducks. Many experts understand the personalities of Mallard ducks are are more than willing to comply.

Building a relationship with your waterfowl expert is extremely crucial when you own Mallard ducks. Your expert takes up the responsibility to ensure that your ducks are healthy from the moment you bring them home. He checks them for any bacterial or viral infections that they could spread into their surroundings. He then examines them for any visible ailments, defects or injuries that can be fixed. Your expert is also able to rightly determine your Mallard duck's gender for you and advise you on the best ways to care for your duck.

It is always wise to find your waterfowl expert before your bring your Mallard ducks home, so they can be examined as soon as you buy them. This simple precautionary action on your part will help you and your expert prevent any unnecessary ailments from befalling either your ducks or you.

Treating a Broken Wing

A Mallard duck takes great pride in its wings, seeing as it forms an integral part of the duck's identity. A broken wing, therefore, is arguably one of the most traumatic episodes that a Mallard duck may experience. Injury to the duck's wing inhibits such routine activities as walking, swimming, running or even standing, causing great stress to its well-being. And if you're a duck owner who is ethically against practices like pinioning or feather clipping, understand that wing injury can be as adversely impactful as these methods.

If you're Mallard duck has not already signalled an injury with distress calls, you can spot an injured wing for yourself by its appearance. When injured, a Mallard duck's wing tends to hang on the duck's body at an odd, drooping angle. You will also find that the broken wing is visibly asymmetrical to the wing on the other side.

A broken or injured wing could be caused due to a variety of reasons, the most common of them being aggressive behaviour among the flock. Mallard drakes especially will look to damage their competitors' wings to gain dominance. Sometimes, these acts of aggression can become so uncontrollable that Mallard drakes will accidentally injure the female in their rush to be the first to mate with her.

If all is well among your ducks, a broken wing could then be traced to a predatory attack. Used as a powerful tool of defence, it is the wings that predators look to attack in order to maim and weaken a Mallard duck. Other anomalies such as tears and cuts in the wire fencing, or stray sharp tree branches may also injure the duck's wing. No matter how your Mallard duck may have been hurt, as soon as you spot an injured wing, inform your waterfowl expert in order to get your duck immediate attention. While you wait for this medical assistance, there are steps you can take to help calm your duck, stabilize the wound and prevent the injury from worsening:

1. To provide first-aid to your Mallard duck, you have to calm it down and convince it to take your help. An injured Mallard duck reacts to this stressful event by becoming extremely hostile, and will not want to be held or handled.

2. To calm your duck down, gain their trust by placing their feed and fresh water within easy reach, and give the duck some space. When the duck begins feeding, it is usually a safe sign that the duck has calmed down enough that it can be approached.

3. Not all ducks are as easily pacified. In many cases, your duck will refuse to stay still due to its distress and in these instances; the only way to calm your duck is to lift him yourself. Remember, your duck has an injured wing, and so will not move as efficiently as usual. Use this advantage to gently corner your duck so you can lift and examine its wing.

4. The best spots to corner your duck are ones in which he will calm down easily. Such spots include nesting and feeding zones - areas familiar to the duck.

5. When you do lift your duck, hold the injured side away from your body, and gingerly inspect the wing area for visible tears or lacerations.

6. Any wounds that you do spot should be cleaned immediately. You can use the antibacterial wash suggested by your waterfowl expert, or even opt for an iodine wash or a bath with mildly warm water.

7. In case your waterfowl expert does not arrive by this point, or you have to address the injury yourself, you must prepare yourself to create a splint for your duck's wing. This is to help your duck receive some support for its wing while it recovers.

8. The most important reason behind providing support for the wing is to help it heal back to its earlier state. For this you have to gently hold the wing back in its natural position against your duck's body. It is important that your touch be as painless as possible.

9. Now, get out a roll of gauze and wrap its securely around your duck enclosing the wing within. When you bring the gauze over the other side, wrap it under the

uninjured wing. This will allow the duck to have some kind of control over its movement and help lower its stress levels.

10. You can fasten the gauze with pieces of strong tape, or even wrap a layer of tape around the gauze to ensure that its stays put.

11. While the purpose of the gauze and tape is preventing the duck from moving its wing, ensure that you don't wrap it on too tightly. This may constrict the Mallard duck's body and make it difficult for the duck to breathe.

12. Mallard ducks with injured wings recover best when kept in nesting zones by themselves. They will make a full recovery in about 4 weeks, provided you give keep them fed and rested.

13. You may notice that the protective gauze has become dirty or soiled; you can change the dressing if you wish. Usually, owners will change the dressing after the first week or two. If you take off the dressing during this point and find your duck exercising its wing comfortably, take it to mean that your pet has healed.

14. Once the Mallard duck is flapping and waddling about confidently, they will automatically socialize with the others in their flock. This is a healthy sign that your duck has made a complete recovery.

Not all wing injuries may be this procedural or easy to fix. In case the wound looks too deep, or has been caused due to a predatory attack, it is best that you seek immediate help from your veterinarian.

Treating Attacks from Predators

Mallard ducks have a few tricks at their disposal to help them evade capture from predators in their area. Furthermore, if you have provided the right kind of nesting and sheltering spaces, your Mallard ducks should be at minimum risk of harm. Despite your best efforts, however, you may not always be able to avoid predatory attacks.

Predatory Terrain	Common Predators
Terrestrial predators	Snakes, foxes, dogs, wolves, coyotes, weasels, minks, bobcats, opossums, raccoons, dingoes, skunks, rats, badgers, ferrets, cats, bears
Aerial predators	Hawks, falcons, owls, crows, ravens, magpies,
Marine predators	Otters, herons, turtles, crocodiles, frogs, large fish

If you're Mallard duck is not able to escape or is not defended by a bigger creature, there are high possibilities that they may not survive the attack. Often, such injuries as a severed neck, internal bleeding, a ruptured organ, or even the trauma of the attack turn out to be life-threatening for the duck. In the instance that your duck has survived the attack, and has received immediate attention, they can overcome the intensity of the injury with the right care.

The first step you have to take is to provide first-aid for the duck's wounds. Your waterfowl expert will recommend that you stock an antibacterial wash for the injuries; use this to clean the affected areas. If you do not have any wash at hand, clean water will suffice. During this wash, gently check your Mallard duck for any fractures, sprains, or injuries that may seem even slightly painful. Address these concerns by either taking the duck to the waterfowl expert at once, or asking them to make an urgent house visit.

Your veterinarian will be able to repair most injuries caused due to predatory attacks. Once his job is done, it is up to you and your Mallard duck to ensure that your pet makes a complete recovery. During the healing stage, Mallard ducks are highly vulnerable to infections and post-traumatic stress. To help them recover, try and provide as sterile and comfortable an atmosphere as you can. Coordinate with your waterfowl expert to determine the time of recovery, means of medication and any other factors that can aid your duck's rehabilitation. No matter how traumatic the attack, it is your response to the event that can help save your Mallard duck's life.

Chapter Nine: Breeding Mallard Ducks

If you have brought home and raised a large group of Mallard ducks, you will soon find yourself with more eggs than you can use! As a potential Mallard duck owner, the option to breed Mallard ducks for commercial purposes is one that you must certainly consider.

Breeding Mallard ducks is a different experience when compared to such animals as cows, sheep, horses, dogs, cats or even chickens. Left to their own devices, Mallard ducks function on an efficient social system that allows the drake to mate with multiple females and lay hundreds of eggs each year.

In fact, breeding instincts are so strong among Mallards, that the absence of an eligible drake may prompt the females to engage in same-sex activities that mimic sexual intercourse. Coupled with the easy attitudes of the Mallard

ducks, this bountiful yield gives you plenty of options to make a profit.

1.   Types of Breeding

When you have made the time and found the resources to breed Mallard Ducks for a profit, you come across another important decision - the choice to opt for ducks born through natural or artificial breeding methods.

Through the natural breeding method, Mallard ducks will only breed with members of their own type, in order to maintain a pure genetic code. Through the process of natural selection, however, Mallard duck species over the years have undergone subtle genetic mutations to adapt their bodies evolving environments. When you breed ducks through the natural method, you allow nature to play its part in determining which traits in your ducks are desirable, and which can be eliminated.

You may also opt for artificial breeding, an increasingly popular method of Mallard duck breeding today. This school of breeding gives you control over the traits that you would want your flock to possess. However, successful mutation is an intricate and complicated process, and does not always ensure the results you wished for. Since physical traits seem to be the characteristics most affected by artificial breeding, this option is sensible should you choose to breed duck for exhibitionary and display purposes.

2.   Breeding Mallard Ducks for Exhibition

If your intent for raising the ducks is for husbandry purposes, the plumage and physical appearance of the duck will make no actual difference to the nature of care they require. If you are bringing home and raising Mallard ducks for decorative purposes, however, you will be especially interested in the physical appearance of the ducks.

While wild Mallard ducks have a distinctive plumage, the science of breeding has allowed Mallard duck enthusiasts to rear ducks with startling bursts of plumage that are equally beautiful, yet completely individualistic. Since the endless possibilities that breeding provides may give an unfair advantage to some experienced individuals over others, most poultry associations that judge decorative competitions only accept those Mallard ducks with their natural colorings. For exhibition and personal pleasures, however, you can choose from increasingly diverse range of available Mallard birds.

A drawback of having diverse color patterns among Mallard ducks is the confusion that arises when they are to be identified. If you plan on bringing home Mallard ducks, it is important that you have a basic understanding of the role that genetic factors play in determining the appearance of these birds.

3.   Genetics and the Mallard duck appearance

The DNA structure in living beings controls every aspect of development - from physical traits, to mental progress and even emotional tendencies. Mallard ducks are not exempt from this natural phenomenon, and pass down inherent characteristics embedded into their genetic codes through the generations.

Because the physical coats Mallard ducks are so diversely patterned and colored, the genetic structure of their code can be modified to produce different results in resulting

Mallard duck generations. Through these modifications, breeders have the option of emphasising those traits that they find desirable, while submitting those traits that they find negative or unwelcome.

The process of genetic modification does not only take place in the laboratories; this is a natural evolutionary process that has resulted in contemporary wild Mallards still differing from their direct ancestors. Abrupt abnormalities in genetic mutations can also occur when an entire flock or more of ducks are affected by a similar tweak in their code. An instance of this mutation has been observed in wild Mallard ducks who grow larger than regular Mallards and display no white patterns on their wings.

In order to pass down genetic traits, the sex cells of each parent fuse to provide half the structure required for the genetic code of the hatchling. A Mallard hatchling, therefore, will contain a gene copy received from the mother and father. Since the final cell is fused using only half of the parent genes, the duckling's cell may either be composed of two similar cells - making them homozygous, or two different cells - rendering them heterozygous.

It is this homozygous or heterozygous nature that determines the spread and distribution of physical and sexual traits in the duckling. If the duckling carries similar version of both cells, it will naturally display the dominant traits it has received. If the duckling receives two different genes codes, however, it will display the mutations of the more dominant set of traits, resulting in a variety of physical patterns and colorations.

4.   The Advantages of Breeding

If you are curious about the advantages that Mallard duck husbandry can have, you are in for a pleasant surprise! It may take considerable time, work and dedication on your part, but Mallard duck husbandry is not unmanageable, mainly due to the following benefits:

1. Mallard ducks are among the least demanding of all poultry. Unlike other species of ducks, chicken, turkeys etc., Mallard ducks are content to mingle among their own kind and rarely require your undivided attention.

2. Mallard ducks are fairly resilient to many forms of poisoning, illness and infection. Apart from the odd medical expenses, you can ensure your ducks' health by simply maintaining the right settings.

3. Mallard ducks are also among the most adaptable of all avian creatures. As long as their needs of constant food, water, resting and nesting spaces are met, Mallard ducks will find a way to adjust to a varying range of climates and housing conditions.

4. Mallard ducks possess a calmer demeanour than most of their aviary counterparts. With a fondness for routine and habits, Mallard ducks are at their happiest quietly foraging for food or interacting with other ducks. They only exhibit brief moments of aggression during the mating season, and even these urges can be tamed.

5. Young ducklings, possessing the traits that adult Mallard ducks do, make for ideal nurturing companions. With few demands, and a relatively hassle-free development, Mallard ducks are among the easiest animals to bring home and raise.

6. And finally, your adult Mallards will reward your nurturing settings by providing you more eggs than other poultry sources. Since the average Mallard duck lays up to 10 eggs a day at the peak of the mating season, you can expect a healthy yield of around 150 eggs per female duck in one season.

Chapter Ten: Caring for Mallard Hatchlings and Eggs

If you are planning to adopt and domestic a flock of Mallard ducks, you have to be prepared for the duck eggs the females will inevitably lay. By the time your Mallard ducks reach full maturity, you will have formed enough of a bond to decide what to do with these duck eggs. A popular option that could also be profitable is to sell the eggs. You may also choose to let the eggs hatch and raise the hatchlings as your own. In either case, handling Mallard ducks eggs is a large responsibility, and proper care can greatly affect the quality of your duck eggs, as well as the health of the hatchlings.

The Importance of Nesting

When your Mallard ducks reach seven months of age, the females begin to look for nesting spots to lay their eggs. If you plan on using the eggs for either breeding or profit, it becomes essential to provide them with the perfect spaces to nest. When left in the wild, Mallard ducks like to scatter their eggs in areas that are grassy, or have hollow openings and hidden nooks away from predatory eyes.

When you determine the nesting space for your duck, you can either choose to enclose an area and allow the ducks to roam freely within it, or construct a specific nesting-and-brooding box. The simplest of these nesting boxes consist of simple crates or boxes incubated with lots of straw and cosy material. The more elaborate consist of settings that mimic the Mallard duck's natural surroundings. While you can set up your nesting zone to your convenience, ensure that the following factors are taken care of:

1. Your nesting space should be in a dark, private and quiet part of your home, as this helps the ducks feel safe enough to lay their eggs. Provide privacy by construction cozy dark nooks around your nesting zone.

2. Your nesting box doesn't necessarily need to have a bottom, especially if you can place it on surfaces such as grass, bare earth or floors covered with wooden shavings and straw. If you do provide a bottom for your zone, ensure that it is enough insulation material such as straw for the duck to nest comfortably.

3. A larger space also helps the ducks feel less claustrophobic and puts them at ease. Areas such as shady trees or the corner of fences at the back of your house are good locations as they provide natural protection from predators, along with privacy.

4. It is essential that your nesting zone remain as free from moisture and humidity as possible. This will help keep the nesting zone fresh and free from bacterial and fungal infestations. A dry area with lots of air flow provides the perfect setting for nesting.

5. If you have multiple Mallard ducks, they may become competitive over certain nesting zones. In these cases, it is better to build more nesting zones that you have female eggs to ensure that every female duck is happy!

Features of a Mallard duck egg

The quality of your Mallard duck egg depends on a variety of factors ranging from the environment your duck lives into the nutritional content of its feed. Provided that you raise you flock of Mallard ducks in the right conditions, the average Mallard duck egg should have a smooth, unblemished shell whose colour will be between a pale grey to a muddy green. A healthy egg should measure about 5 to 6.5cms long, and between 3.9 and 4.5cms wide.

Whether you choose to sell the duck eggs for a profit, or use them to replenish your own food source, understand that Mallard duck eggs provide high levels of nutrition. A Mallard duck egg is a bountiful source of vitamins and minerals as vitamins A, B6, B12, D, E, iron, potassium, phosphorous, calcium and zinc.

In addition, a Mallard duck egg provides essential amino acids and 7.3gms of healthy Omega-rich fats, essential for daily sustenance. Finally, a Mallard duck egg provides between 100 and 110 calories of your daily intake, while supplying you with 9.3gms of protein and a little over 600 mg of cholesterol.

Dealing with the Eggs

Mallard ducks are generally ready to lay eggs by the time they are seven months old. If you have provided the right nesting conditions, a female Mallard duck will sit in preferred spots and begin to lay an egg per day almost immediately. What happens with the eggs from that point is your choice to make.

You have one of two options to choose at this stage - either allow the eggs to hatch into ducklings or use the eggs as a food source for profit or personal use. Initially, many Mallard duck breeders choose to simply observe how their ducks incubate and hatch their eggs. This is a wise option, as it allows you to study and determine how you'd like to use the eggs based on the yield.

You may not want to breed the ducks or use their eggs for any purpose. This is perfectly fine, but it will also require some work on your part to prevent the eggs from hatching. If making an egg nonviable is your choice, stay alert to the time that your duck leaves its nest each day to wash and feed itself. When she is busy, make your way to the eggs, lift and shake each one, before placing them back.

The act of shaking the egg damages the delicate contents and blood vessels within, putting a stop to the development process. To prevent your duck form further laying eggs, it is essential that you place the shaken eggs back in place. If your duck can't find her eggs upon return, she'll simply lay a fresh batch.

a.   Collecting the eggs for profit

If you have chosen to use the Mallard ducks eggs for profit, you simply have to pick the eggs up once they are hatched. If you choose to pick the eggs one at a time, you may spend all day simply collecting eggs. It is smarter to wait till all the eggs have been laid for the day, and collect them together, since development only begins after all the eggs are laid.

Since Mallard ducks are known to be among the more superior of domestic aviary birds, expect to find eggs that are considerably larger in size and denser in mass. It is due to their high-quality nutritional value that Mallard duck eggs are prized food sources for predators such as foxes, dogs, weasels and raccoon. While the mother will stay and defend her eggs against smaller predators, she will likely abandon the eggs when confronted with a larger animal.

If the Mallard duck's eggs are of importance to you, it is wise to provide an enclosed and secure space for your female ducks, especially during the breeding season. If you have set up a free-range style of housing for the ducks, you can construct a temporary "bedroom" to house the females at night. This keeps their eggs protected from stealthy attacks by predators during the quieter hours. You can also ensure better protection for your ducks by training a guard dog for this purpose.

b.   Collecting the eggs for breeding

If you have provided the right incubation conditions for your Mallard ducks, expect to be pleasantly surprised with the yield! At the peak of the breeding season, you will get between 8 and 10 eggs per female duck per day. This yield, at the end of the laying season can total up to a healthy average of 150 Mallard duck eggs a year! It is important to understand, however, that attaining all the eggs that have been laid may not always be possible. A variety of factors determine how many eggs you can actually collect and how many of these can be either sold or hatched successfully.

If collecting the Mallard duck eggs is your goal, remember that the ducks will not lay eggs at their nests alone. In a comfortable atmosphere, Mallard ducks are likely to wander around, laying their eggs at any spot they see fit. This means that you have to exercise great caution while looking for eggs, to avoid damaging any before you collect them. Damage could also be caused by other ducks or animals in your space, so it is crucial that you collect the eggs soon after they are laid.

Mallard ducks generally prefer the quiet hours of the day to lay their eggs - between the last hours of the night and the early hours of the morning. Therefore, it makes best sense to collect the eggs early during the day. Ensure that you carry a plastic egg tray to deposit the eggs into, taking care to store the cleaner ones away from the those with a dirtier shell. It also helps to give your Mallard duck a two-hour window after dawn to ensure she lays no more eggs for the day.

As you go about collecting your eggs, examine them for cracks, irregularities on the shell or inconsistencies in the appearance. The healthy Mallard ducks should be as close as possible in appearance to the description of the egg above. The more deformities in the Mallard duck egg, the less it is likely to hatch into a healthy duckling. This egg examination, therefore, is crucial in case you're planning to start your Mallard duck flock.

All those Mallard duck eggs that pass your critical examination then need to be hygienic and clean. Plenty of unhealthy microbial life is likely to be present on the shells, and if not cleaned away, may seep into the yolk through the tiniest crack on the egg. Your best options to clean the egg without damaging its fragile exterior are to use a piece of steel wool or even a damp cloth.

Wipe down your egg gently without applying too much pressure, and do not wash it under any circumstances! Washing has been observed to have negative effects on the hatching process. If you are extremely picky about the hygiene of the eggs, you can also try basic fumigation. Simply wipe down your eggs with a mixture of potassium permanganate and formalin to clean the area of dangerous bacteria.

Hatching the Eggs

Should you choose to have your Mallard duck eggs hatch into little ducklings, determine the process by which you'd like the hatchlings to emerge. Since Mallard ducks are famed for their egg laying abilities, you will receive anywhere between 150 and 200 eggs a year. It may not be possible for your duck to hatch all these eggs by herself successfully. Working with your Mallard duck, you can provide optimum incubation conditions - natural or artificial - to hatch as many healthy ducklings as possible.

a. Natural Incubation

The most obvious choice for incubation of your Mallard duck eggs would be through the natural method - having the duck hatch the eggs herself. A female Mallard duck likes to collectively nest and hatch her eggs. To facilitate this, she stops laying eggs at a certain time during the day and prepares herself to physically place herself over the eggs. This process, called brooding, is part of a Mallard duck's daily routine.

To signal that she is ready to brood, a female Mallard duck will let out a peculiar, yet distinct sound, accompanied by a halt in egg-laying. If you have provided a specific nesting zone for your duck, it is here that she will lay the eggs and then return to brood.

All the eggs receive a uniform amount of warmth and moisture from the duck when there are less than 15 eggs in the same spot. Once the duck plants herself over this group of eggs, it takes around a week for the hatchlings to begin development. At the end of this week, you can determine whether the egg is fertile by holding it against a bright light source. A fertile egg will have visible matter on the inside, while an infertile one will appear clear.

Since your duck spends all her time with the eggs, you have to ensure that she is provided with food and water at the right times. It is also essential that the incubation space is as dry and clean as possible, and as in a quiet and secure space.

b. Artificial Incubation

Brooding is a process undertaken by the Mallard duck when she can find the eggs she has laid during the day. If you collect the Mallard duck's eggs in her absence at the end of each day, her brooding instincts will diminish and even disappear altogether. When you collect the eggs with the purpose of hatching them, however, artificial incubation becomes essential.

The entire process of incubation takes about 28 days, and you can find many commercially manufactured incubators that correctly serve this purpose. Incubating Mallard duck eggs is a tricky procedure that requires specific temperature and humidity settings. Commercial incubators solve this problem by allowing you to regulate conditions with an inbuilt thermostat.

The most interesting feature of artificial incubators is that they allow you to hatch many eggs at once. Since the eggs themselves take around a month to hatch, it is wise to collect many eggs before incubating them together. Duck eggs can keep for approximately seven days before incubation, provided they are stored in the right conditions. Optimum conditions for duck egg storage are a temperature of 13 degrees Celsius with a humidity percentage of 75.

Once you have a sufficient number of stored eggs, place them at room temperature for around 6 hours before you shift them into the incubator. This will prepare the eggs for the heightened conditions within the incubating space, which should be set to 37.5 degrees Celsius at humidity percentage of 70.Towards the end of the incubation process, you should reduce the temperature by 0.2 degrees for optimum hatching. Check for fertilized and developing eggs the same way you would check eggs in the natural incubation method.

Throughout the incubation process, you should turn the eggs at about 90 degrees multiple times every day to prevent the contents from sticking to the shell. In case you have too many eggs and the process is too tedious, you can find equipment that will turn your eggs for you!

Caring for a newly hatched duckling

Even though you may undertake the incubation process with utmost care and caution, you still should not be disappointed if all the eggs don't hatch. Mallard duck eggs, have a 70 per cent rate of hatching, and for a hatchling to successfully emerge from incubation, it has to first be shifted to a brooder.

Brooding zones for hatchlings are critical to their survival, where they have hatched through the artificial or natural incubation method. You should shift the hatchlings into the brooder almost as soon as they hatch. While it is tricky to determine the exact moment of hatching, a Mallard duck mother will signal the hatching period by spending less time sitting on the eggs. When she spends almost no time with the eggs at all, you know they're ready to crack!

New-born hatchlings survive best when fed with specially-raised farmer pellets, prepared to contain all the necessary nutrients. Tougher form of food, such as grit, is safe to feed the ducklings once they're over a month old.

There is no hard evidence that advocates one method of hatching over the other. While the natural way seems like the best hatching technique, artificial incubation has also met with great success. The final choice truly comes down your individual settings, preferences and expectations from your flock of ducks.

Factors affecting your Mallard duck's egg laying habits

If you have raised your Mallard ducks with the specific purpose of using their eggs, you will, at some point, find differences in the egg-laying habits of your ducks. There may be a shift in the frequency, or your ducks may not be laying any eggs at all. In case your duck has developed certain ailments or reproductive disorders, a check-up with your local expert should help isolate the cause. In many cases, however, several natural and environmental factors may combine to affect the way a perfectly healthy duck lays their eggs, such as:

1. The age of your bird

Even though Mallard ducks may be prolific breeders, their reproductive abilities do diminish as they age, with their egg-laying possibly coming to a full stop in the last stages of their lives.

2. Unfavourable weather conditions

As we have seen, successful egg-laying depends on favourable weather conditions. If the area is not warm enough, or airy enough for the Mallard ducks, they will find it difficult to be comfortable enough to lay eggs.

3. Fluctuations and irregularities in daily routine

Mallard ducks are disciplined creatures by nature and thrive on routine and habits. Any fluctuations in their daily feeding, cleaning or handling schedule will confuse the ducks and prevent them from finding a suitable time to lay their eggs each day. Mallard ducks, in fact, require so much structure that changes to the contents of their daily feed is also likely to cause them stress.

4. Parasites and predators in the environment

If you're Mallard ducks feel threatened by any predatory sources in their surroundings, they will become highly paranoid and stressed. As a defence mechanism, they may stop laying eggs altogether.

5. Arrival of new ducks

Mallard ducks may be disciplined, but they also possess highly social and interactive natures. If you introduce new ducks to the flock just before the nesting season, you tend to disturb the already established pecking order (a result of their rigid and disciplined nature). Mallard ducks are then unlikely to resume laying eggs until the new ducks have been properly integrated into the community and the pecking order has been modified and re-established.

6. Ready to brood

Brooding is perhaps the biggest factor that may cause your duck to stop laying eggs, but it is often that duck-owners have least knowledge of. Mallard ducks prefer to lay all their eggs first, and then nest them together at a time. If your duck has suddenly stopped laying eggs, she could just be looking for those that you collected. With time, Mallard ducks adjust to their disappearing eggs and simply lay new ones when they can't find their eggs anymore. Therefore, brooding is a habit that will occur more commonly among newer, younger mothers.

No matter what the causal factor, a sudden slump or halt in laying eggs is not enough to classify your Mallard duck as infertile. It is, in fact, necessary that you reassess your husbandry practices, along with the factors in the duck's environment thoroughly, to ensure that your duck receives the kind of care that allow it to lay eggs well past its prime.

Maximizing your Mallard duck's egg-laying potential

Once you begin collecting eggs, and see for yourself how much you can gain from either breeding or using the eggs for profit, you may obviously want to yield as many eggs as possible from the Mallard ducks. Through some easy measures, you can ensure that your ducks provide the most amounts of healthy eggs they can.

a. Control the lighting conditions

The most important feature that ensures consistent egg-laying is proper and consistent lighting: Mallard ducks are the most sexually active during the months of January and June, when the days are relatively longer. For the Mallard duck to lay the maximum eggs in a day, she requires about 17 hours of constant light. This is evidently not possible with natural lighting, so you will have to make artificial lighting arrangements.

With prepared lighting sources, understand that you cannot increase the exposure to light by a great amount overnight. Ducks require stable condition to be comfortable, so increase the exposure to light by about half an hour daily, at the start and end of the day, till you reach 17 hours in a few days' time.

b. Regulate the feed

Along with adequate lighting, the nature of the feed is crucial in determining the frequency and quality of the Mallard duck eggs. There are plenty of food choices available for your duck in the market today, so be as fussy as you can. Ensure that the feed contains all the nutrients your ducks may need, and that the feed is as fresh as possible. Any bacterial or fungal growth on the feed will adversely affect the health of the duck as well.

Apart from the quality of the feed, you also have to ensure that the feed is appropriate for the age of your duck. The bills and digestive systems of your Mallard ducklings are far more sensitive than their adult counterparts, and they must be fed appropriately. The amount of the food you supply the ducks plays an equally important role.

Nesting Mallard ducks require a constant supply of food, but this supply needs to be of the same quantity. Overweight or underweight ducks will probably develop health issues that will interfere with fertility and reproduction. Ideally, .35 pounds of feed changed daily should be adequate for your Mallard duck.

c. Ensure a constant supply of fresh water

Ducks, being semi-aquatic creatures, require a source of water for them to thrive and reproduce. This water not only provides them with a drinking source, but also helps them exercise and keep their bodily temperatures regulated.
Since Mallard ducks are sticklers for hygiene and cleanliness, the quality of the water is essential. Muddy water filled with debris will prove to be a stressful atmosphere for your ducks, while a clean source of running water will prove to be the most beneficial.

d. Keep the Mallard drakes to a minimum

Due to the social nature of Mallard ducks, the composition of drakes in proportion to female ducks is crucial in maintaining a peaceful and sexually active environment. Ideally, one Mallard duck is sufficient for a group of 5 female ducks. Any more drakes in the flock will lead to competition among the males for dominance.

This competition can prove to be both harmful and stressful for the females, who may stop laying eggs in response. Ensure that you maintain a 1:5 ratio of Mallard drakes to female ducks for a healthy environment.

e. Stress-free ducks lay the most eggs!

Ducks in general, and Mallard ducks in particular, are extremely fond of schedules and order. Their daily routines are determined by a specific amount of food, drink, activity and rest with standardized timings for each activity.

Furthermore, Mallard ducks are also extremely sensitive to lighting conditions, climatic changes, new locations and even new people. Therefore, maintain as strict a routine as you can with your Mallard ducks. The familiarity will put them at ease and allow them to lay eggs in a comfortable and secure space.

The choice to breed and rear ducks is one that requires great commitment, time and patience. To get the most out of your breeding experience, it is essential that you integrate yourself into the lives of your flock. Once you learn the ways of your ducks, the care-taking process becomes easier and comforting, both for you and your Mallard ducks.

There is plenty of help available, should you require it while breeding your Mallard ducks. Do not hesitate to consult your local waterfowl expert with any queries regarding your ducks, eggs, or the ducklings.

Above all, understand that breeding Mallard ducks for profit is a process that is time consuming. You have to be extremely patient and diligent in your efforts. As long as you can provide and maintain a healthy and sustained environment for your Mallard ducks, you will find this experience to be not only profitable, but also rewarding.

Resources

Seek to continually learn more about your Mallard ducks. As with the husbandry of all domestic animals, new techniques and strategies are developed constantly. Never turn down an opportunity to learn more about your new pets, and eagerly seek out those who may know more than you do about these big, beautiful birds.

Books

Books can provide information not found on internet chat rooms and message boards. Books are an especially valuable resource for finding biological information about the species.

Ducks, Geese and Swans: Species Accounts
Edited by Janet Kear
Oxford University Press, 2005
Diseases of Wild Waterfowl
By Gary A. Wobeser
Springer, 1997
Naturalized Birds of the World
By Christopher Lever
A&C Black 2010
Diseases of Poultry
Edited by David E. Swayne
John Wiley & Sons, 2013
Ducks and Geese: Standard Breeds and Management
By George Ellsworth Howard
U.S. Department of Agriculture, 1897
Biology of Breeding Poultry
By Paul M. Hocking
CABI, 2009
Mallard Ducks
By F. Bauer

Papua New Guinea, Department of Primary Industry, 1980

Websites

In the information age, learning more about your Mallard ducks is only a few clicks away. Be sure to bookmark these sites for quick access in the future.

Informational Websites

Backyard Chickens
http://www.backyardchickens.com/
Though focused on chickens, this website and message board contains plenty of information about Mallard ducks as well.
Poultry Hub
http://www.poultryhub.org/
Maintained by the Poultry Cooperative Research Centre, Poultry Hub provides information regarding all aspects of duck care.
Madeira Birdwatching
http://www.madeirabirds.com/
Madeira Birdwatching provides information about the birds commonly seen on the island, including Mallard ducks.
South Florida Mallard Ducks
http://www.southfloridaMallardducks.com/
This site includes information about wild, feral and captive Mallard ducks.
Mallard Duck Central
http://www.Mallardduckcentral.com/
Information about the care and breeding of Mallard ducks.
Backyard Poultry
http://www.backyardpoultrymag.com/
Online magazine featuring news, information and more concerning Mallard ducks and other common poultry.
Ducks Unlimited

http://www.ducks.org/
The world's leading conservation organization dedicated to protecting ducks and their natural habitats.
Cornell Lab of Ornithology
http://www.birds.cornell.edu/
Information about most birds native to North America. This site provides identification photos, sample calls from most species and tips for spotting various species in the wild.
The Poultry Club of Great Britain
http://www.poultryclub.org/
This website provides a variety of helpful resources, as well as information about poultry husbandry and breeding. You can also use this website to find information on breed standards, competitions and meet other poultry enthusiasts.
Xeno-Canto
http://www.xeno-canto.org/
Based in the Netherlands, xeno-canto is a repository for birds sounds, collected from around the world.
Beauty of Birds
http://beautyofbirds.com/
Beauty of Birds has information on Mallard ducks, including information about feral colonies.
The Bird Hotline
http://www.birdhotline.com/
A wealth of information is available on this site. While most is oriented towards parakeets and similar birds, the veterinary resources provided on the website are of value to Mallard keepers.

Breeders

Mallard duck breeders are not only an excellent source for purchasing hatchlings; they can also provide a wealth of information.
The Ugly Duck Farm

Resources

http://Mallard.us/
The Ugly Duck Farm produces birds, and provides information on their website for understanding Mallard duck genetics and health problems.
Al's Quackery
http://alsquackery.weebly.com/
Al's Quackery has plentiful information regarding Mallard duck care and color mutations. Additionally, the Quakery offers Mallard ducks for sale when they are available.
J. M. Hatchery
http://www.jmhatchery.com/
J. M. Hatchery breeds and sells a variety of poultry species, including white Mallard ducks.
CaliforniaHatchery.com
http://www.californiahatchery.com/
CaliforniaHatchery.com sells a wide variety of ducks, chickens and other poultry.
Cheap Chicks Poultry Farm
http://cheapchickpoultryfarm.weebly.com/
Cheap Chicks Poultry Farm sells hatchlings and eggs of Mallard ducks and many other poultry breeds.
Metzer Farms
http://www.metzerfarms.com/
Metzer Farms hatches a variety of bird species, and their website provides information about Mallard housing, maintenance and feeding.

University and Governmental Resources

University of Texas at El Paso
https://www.utep.edu/
The University of Texas, El Paso website contains a great deal of duck-oriented information. Of special note are the bird taxonomy resources, which provide information about the classification of ducks.
University of California, Davis

http://animalscience.ucdavis.edu/
UC Davis works extensively with livestock (including poultry), and they work to enhance the lives of captive and companion animals through science.
Duck Research Laboratory
http://www.duckhealth.com/
Maintained by the Cornell University College of Veterinary Medicine, this site provides a wealth of information regarding the husbandry of ducks, including Mallard ducks.
The Poultry Site
http://www.thepoultrysite.com/
Although primarily focused on turkeys and chickens, this Oklahoma State University maintained website contains some information about Mallard ducks.
Animal Diversity Web
http://animaldiversity.ummz.umich.edu/
Maintained by the University of Michigan, the Animal Diversity Web has thousands of pages of information, detailing the lives of various animal species. In addition to reading about Mallard ducks, you can also learn about their predators, prey and competitors here.
Center for Integrated Agricultural Systems
http://www.cias.wisc.edu/
This page, provided and maintained by the University of Wisconsin-Madison, contains a wealth of data concerning all common farm animals, including Mallard ducks.
The Centers for Disease Control and Prevention
http://www.cdc.gov/
Based in Atlanta, Georgia, the CDC provides information on a variety of diseases that may be zoonotic. Additionally, the website provides further resources for coping with outbreaks of salmonella.

Resources

Veterinary Resources

Veterinarians.com
http://www.localvets.com/
This site is a search engine that can help you find a local veterinarian to treat your Mallard Ducks.
European Committee of the Association of Avian Veterinarians
http://www.eaavonline.org/
This website includes a veterinarian locator, as well as a long list of links that may be useful for Mallard owners.
All About Birds
www.allaboutbirds.org/guide/mallard/id
A comprehensive website that covers various subjects like life history, care and breeding of different domestic birds.
NC Wildlife
www.ncwildlife.org/portals/0/Learning/documents/Profiles/mallard.pdf
A special compilation of Mallard Duck facts and figures.
AvianBiotech.com
http://www.avianbiotech.com/Index.htm
AvianBiotech.com provides DNA-based lab services to bird owners.
Association of Avian Veterinarians
http://www.aav.org/
In addition to being a good resource for finding a qualified avian veterinarian, this site provides information on veterinary colleges, bird health and basic care.
For The Birds
http://www.forthebirdsdvm.com/
Veterinary and care information for all birds, as well as specific care advice for ducks.

Resources

References

Centres for Disease Control and Prevention .(2014). http://www.cdc.gov/features/salmonellapoultry/. Retrieved from CDC.gov:

http://www.cdc.gov/features/salmonellapoultry/
• Enzo R. Campagnolo, M. B. (2001). An Outbreak of Duck Viral Enteritis (Duck Plague) in Domestic Mallard Ducks (Cairinamoschatadomesticus) in Illinois. Avian Diseases.
• Fernando GogliAntoniaLanni, C. D.-L. (1993). Effect of cold acclimation on oxidative capacity and respiratory properties of liver and muscle mitochondria in ducklings, Cairinamoschata.Comparative Biochemistry and Physiology Part B: Comparative Biochemistry.
• GALT, R. J. (1980). MORTALITY IN MALLARD DUCKS (Cairinamoschata) CAUSED BY Haemoproteus INFECTION. Journal of Wildlife Diseases.
• Hilary S. Stern, D. (2014). Care and Feeding of Pet Ducks. Retrieved from For The Birds: http://www.forthebirdsdvm.com/pages/care-and-feeding-of-pet-ducks
• KATARZYNA KLECZEK, E. W.-W. (2007). Effect of body weights of day-old Mallard ducklings on growths .Arch. Tierz., Dummerstorf.
• Kear, J. (2005). Ducks, Geese and Swans: Species accounts (Cairina to Mergus).Oxford University Press.
• Lack, D. (n.d.). The proportion of yolk in the eggs of waterfowl.Wildfowl.
• Larry R. McDougald, P. (2012). Overview of Coccidiosis in Poultry. Retrieved from The Merck Veterinary Manual: http://www.merckmanuals.com/vet/poultry/coccidiosis/ove rview_of_coccidiosis_in_poultry.html

• Mail, D. (2012). That's quite a bill! Prize-winning Mallard drake becomes Britain's most expensive duck after fetching £1,500 at auction .Daily Mail.

• Major Viral Diseases of Waterfowl and Their Control. (2011). Retrieved from The Poultry Site: http://www.thepoultrysite.com/articles/2051/major-viral-diseases-of-waterfowl-and-their-control

• Mutinelli, I. C. (2001). Mortality in Mallard ducks (Cairinamoschata) and domestic geese (Anseranser var. domestica) associated with natural infection with a highly pathogenic avian influenza virus of H7N1 subtype. Avian Pathology .

• Nakamine M, O. M. (1992). The first outbreak of fowl cholera in Mallard ducks (Cairinamoschata) in Japan.The Journal of Veterinary Medical Science / the Japanese Society of Veterinary Science.

• S. Davison, K. A. (1993). Duck Viral Enteritis in Domestic Mallard Ducks in Pennsylvania. Avian Diseases.

• SORENSO, K. P. (1999). PHYLOGENY AND BIOGEOGRAPHY OF DABBLING DUCKS (GENUS: ANAS): A COMPARISON OF MOLECULAR AND MORPHOLOGICAL EVIDENCE .The Auk .

• Stai, S. M. (2004). Promiscuity and sperm competition in Mallard ducks, Cairinamoschata. University of Miami Library.

• That's quite a bill! Prize-winning Mallard drake becomes Britain's most expensive duck after fetching £1,500 at auction .(2012). Daily Mail.

• Tzschentke, B., &Nichelmann, M. (2000). Influence of age and wind speed on total effective ambient temperature in three poultry species

CPSIA information can be obtained
at www.ICGtesting.com
Printed in the USA
BVHW062103300620
582537BV00006B/483